LESTER PEARSON
Diplomat and Politician

Bruce Thordarson

Toronto
OXFORD UNIVERSITY PRESS
1974

ISBN 0-19-540225-1

© Oxford University Press (Canadian Branch) 1974

1 2 3 4 5 6 - 9 8 7 6 5 4

68032

Printed in Canada by
Web Offset Publications Limited

Contents

Illustrations

Preface

Most Canadians remember Lester Bowles Pearson (1897-1972) as Canada's fourteenth Prime Minister. For five turbulent years, from 1963 to 1968, his minority government weathered a succession of crises ranging from scandals involving its own ministers to the growth of nationalist sentiment in Québec that threatened to destroy the Canadian Confederation. This was, at the same time, a period of significant achievement. The government introduced major social legislation to meet the needs of Canadians in an increasingly urban and impersonal society, and national pride was stimulated by the adoption of a distinctive Canadian flag and by the festivities of Centennial Year, 1967.

It is likely, however, that international historians will remember Pearson more for his contributions on the world stage. During the last years of the Second World War and in the immediate post-war period he was Canada's chief negotiator in the discussions that led to the creation of a new world order. Canada emerged from the war as one of the world's most powerful nations, and Pearson utilized this influence—temporary as it was—to encourage the growth of the United Nations (particularly its economic and social agencies) and NATO as instruments for world peace. As Canada's foreign minister from 1948 to 1957 Pearson achieved international recognition for his participation at the

United Nations in a variety of major crises—Palestine, Korea, and, finally, Suez. For his peacekeeping efforts in the Suez crisis he received the international community's supreme accolade, the Nobel Peace Prize.

This biography does not profess to be definitive. Insufficient time has passed since Pearson's death for many of his contemporaries to set down on paper their own record of events or for official documents to become available. This shortage of first-hand sources is particularly noticeable for the years when Pearson was leader of the Liberal party. The record of his earlier years is more fully documented. Considerable time has passed; the magnitude of the events with which he was involved has led numerous historians to assemble the details; and, above all, Pearson has left us with two volumes of reminiscences dealing with the years 1897 to 1957. These memoirs, entitled *Mike*, contain invaluable material and will be the basis for the first part of the definitive biography that will eventually be written.

Despite the lack of satisfactory sources dealing with the latter part of Pearson's life, there is some value in reviewing from beginning to end the career of such a distinguished Canadian. As no single biographical account of his entire life is available at present, students of the Pearson years are obliged to examine a variety of sources that do not provide continuity. (Young students may not even remember the last and most recent part of Pearson's career.) Many of the sources are either unhesitatingly laudatory or snipingly critical; it is desirable to obtain some kind of balance—or at least to set out as much of the story as is available so that the reader can make his own assessment. In addition, an account of Pearson's life is a useful summary of much recent history, both Canadian and international. It includes the growth of Canada's role in world affairs from its humble origins after the First World War to the 'golden decade' of 1947-57; the development of the post-1945 world order and the major international crises that threatened to lead to another world war; and the raucous 'Diefenbaker-Pearson years' that dominated a decade of Canadian politics from 1957 to 1968.

One theme that will emerge from the account that follows is the effect of Pearson's character on those who came in contact with him. Whatever the assessment of his accomplishments and failures, it is undeniable that he was one of the most likeable public figures in Canadian history. Many of his diplomatic triumphs were due to his unique ability to set people at ease and to win their trust; even when he was later under severe attack as Prime Minister, reporters said privately that they hated to write anything bad about a person as nice as Mike Pearson. His humanity and his inability to take himself too seriously shone through to the university students he taught in Ottawa after his retirement, of whom I was one. It will be some time before a final judgement can be reached about the diplomat and politician, but an assessment of Pearson the man has already been silently made by those who knew him.

Lester Pearson (standing on the chair) with his parents and brothers, about 1900.

1

Background

In 1897 the village of Newtonbrook, several miles north of Toronto, faced the twentieth century with confidence, oblivious of the fact that it was destined to become an anonymous suburb, swallowed up by the growing metropolitan region. It was a time of optimism for the residents of southern Ontario. The little towns that formed a semi-circle around Toronto—Peterborough, Aurora, Willowdale, Davisville, Hamilton, and others—basked serenely in the relative prosperity of rural Ontario. Here the frontier had long since been pushed back; it was towards the western prairies that the swelling tides of immigrants moved in search of homesteads. The towns of southern Ontario—with their wooden frame houses, neatly planted flower-beds, and large back yards—offered their residents a way of life that was simple, unpretentious, and comfortable.

Lester Bowles Pearson was born at the Methodist parsonage in Newtonbrook on April 23, 1897. His mother's family, the Bowles, had come to Canada from Ireland in the 1830s. His grandfather, Thomas Bowles, was a farmer like other members of the family and a lay preacher in the Methodist Church. (Although the church had ordained ministers, it gave a licence to any lay member who desired to preach.) The Pearson side of the family was no less involved in the work of the church. Lester's grandfather and father were both ordained ministers who were assigned to various parishes in the Toronto area. Because the Methodist Church frequently rotated its ministers from town to town, Lester's family moved frequently during his childhood. He received his elementary and high-school education in four towns not far from Toronto: Davisville, Aurora, Peterborough, and Hamilton.

Lester and his two brothers—Marmaduke, who was older, and Vaughan, who was younger—grew up in a household that, while not poor, was nevertheless very simple. While the Pearson family did not go wanting, there was little money available for extras. The average salary of a Methodist minister was around $700 a year, but a house was traditionally provided. The parsonage was usually a big, comfortable dwelling with trees in the front yard and a garden in the back. As sons of the local minister, the Pearson brothers were expected to be on their best behaviour at all times. Cards, tobacco, and alcohol were to be avoided; so was dancing when the boys became old enough to be interested in it. However, Lester's father was not stuffy or sanctimonious. An outgoing man, Edwin Pearson was friendly and got along well with almost everyone; indeed, his wife felt at times that he was too easy-going and too loyal to his favourite philosophy of 'live and let live'. He had inherited from his father, as did Lester and his brothers from him, a love of sports of all kinds. At Sunday School picnics he could usually be found playing first base in a pick-up baseball game. He encouraged his sons to take part in sports, and took them to baseball games in which he played for the local team—a most uncommon practice for a minister of the Methodist Church in those days. Edwin Pearson, who died in 1934, taught his children that rank and riches meant little beside the higher values of sincerity and simplicity. He once advised Lester to be kind and understanding to people he passed on his way up since he would no doubt meet them again on his way down.

Annie Bowles Pearson, Lester's mother, brought a combination of Irish enthusiasm and Methodist strictness to the family. She cheerfully did all the parish duties expected of a minister's wife in addition to the regular chores of bread-baking, soap-making, and washing clothes in the back yard. Writing about her some seventy years later, Lester recalled that she was the centre of the tightly knit family group, 'its soul and solace', and that she filled her children with a sense of security and love. They had a happy, carefree childhood, full of the joys of sports and family companionship, even if Lester did not get the bicycle, the boy scout uniform, or the pair of genuine tube hockey skates for which he longed.

The Pearsons, like other Ontarians of the time, accepted without question Canada's dependence on Great Britain and the importance of the monarchy to the British Empire. One of Lester's vivid recollections of his kindergarten days in Aurora was the evening the whole town gathered at the railway station to greet the Duke of York, heir to the throne, and his Duchess, whose train was to slow down as it passed through Aurora on its way from Toronto. This was the hey-day of imperialist sentiment in Canada. Queen Victoria's diamond jubilee had been an occasion of great celebration in 1897, and two years later Canada had voluntarily sent troops to fight on Britain's side against the Boers in South Africa. There was, as yet, little feeling that Canada's interests were, or should be, distinct from those of Great Britain, the beloved mother country.

During his first few years of school Lester received good

grades but was far from being bookish. Sports—baseball, hockey, and football—were his great love. When he was ten his family was living in Peterborough, where his teacher at Central Public School was R.F. Downey, the man whom he later credited with arousing his intellectual curiosity and making him feel that school was good, not merely a limitation on his freedom. 'He had a way with boys,' Pearson once recalled, 'and he got me interested in work and trying to do well. He got me to see that while it was important to play baseball and make the baseball team, it was important to win a scholarship too, just as much fun as any other competition.' He had similar good fortune at high school in Hamilton, where a teacher named Mike McGarvin aroused in him an interest in history that he never lost. The combination of encouragement from his teachers and parents, plus his own natural intelligence and good memory, led to excellent results in school, and he graduated from Hamilton Collegiate with high honours. He also remained popular with his fellow students because of his great interest in sports and other extra-curricular activities, such as music. He had learned to play the piano at an early age, advancing from Sunday School concert duets with his brother Duke to more difficult classical music by the time he reached high school.

After receiving his senior matriculation from Hamilton Collegiate Institute in 1913 at the age of sixteen, Lester was ready to leave home for university. The family took for granted that he would go to Victoria College, a Methodist foundation at the University of Toronto, where his older brother Duke was already studying. His parents also expected that, after obtaining a B.A. in history, Lester would follow the family tradition and enter the ministry. During his first year at Victoria, Lester shared a room with Duke in the college residence, where he first met Vincent Massey, the dean of residence and a lecturer in history with whom Pearson was to be closely associated in future years. In addition to making friends and playing on several varsity teams, he cultivated an increasingly deep interest in history. In the final examinations he placed first in modern history, which was proving to be his major interest. (He did not fare nearly so well in the more perplexing fields of science and mathematics.) He spent the summer playing baseball in Chatham, where his father had just been transferred. Although hockey was his best sport, his baseball talents were such that he was later able to play in a semi-pro league. A teammate recalled that he was a 'good glove man' at second base, but 'not much of a batter'.

When Pearson returned for his sophomore year in the fall of 1914, the First World War had just broken out. Nevertheless, life went on as usual at Victoria College. He continued to be interested in his studies, won second prize in the college oratorical contest, and played on the college football team. After the Christmas break, however, things changed. The war, which both sides had confidently predicted would be over by Christmas, was turning into a prolonged and bloody battle of attrition. More and more Canadians began to respond to the appeal to enlist, stirred by allied propaganda and stories of 'Hun' atrocities. In March 1915 Duke Pearson joined the growing list of volunteers, and Lester suddenly found their double room very empty and lonely. Beginning to feel that he too must serve in what allied propaganda was depicting as a 'glorious adventure' to save the free world, Lester began drilling with the University Officers Training Corps, since his parents felt he was still too young, at seventeen, to go overseas. One day in April he was in the college library, somewhat bored, studying two Latin authors, when the librarian told him he was wanted on the telephone. It was a call from a friend who had enlisted a few weeks earlier with the University of Toronto Hospital Unit, and who had learned there was a vacancy that Pearson, if he hurried, might be able to fill. Jumping at the opportunity, especially since the friend had told him they might be sent overseas any day, he rushed down to the armouries, enlisted, and was given a uniform. Dressed in khaki, he created quite a stir when he returned to the library to pick up his books. That evening he phoned to obtain the consent of his parents, who reluctantly agreed, realizing that if he was determined to go, it was at least desirable that he should go in a noncombatant role. He was given permission by the university to write his exams before he left and then he was on his way overseas with his unit to participate in what Pearson, like almost everyone else, felt was a 'war to make the world safe for democracy'.

The troop ship was overcrowded; the troops were jammed together in the hold, sleeping and eating side by side. 'We live like cattle,' Pearson noted in a diary he kept. After a bearable voyage down the St Lawrence River and through the Gulf, the week that followed on the high sea was agony. 'For sheer misery,' Pearson wrote in his memoirs, 'nothing was to equal it during all my years of military service. I was homesick. I was seasick as no other human being had ever been. Never again was I to look on the sea—even from a prime-ministerial suite on a luxury liner—with anything but fear and distaste.' The camp near Dover, where Pearson's unit spent the summer, improved his health but did little for his morale. There he received a letter from an aunt in Orangeville, who wrote: 'I can see you now, a ministering angel to the poor men on the battlefield, helping them midst shot and shell.' Little did she know that his activities consisted mainly of scrubbing floors, washing patients, and emptying bedpans. Another letter, however, informed him that he had won the Regent's Prize for the best English essay by a second-year student at Victoria College. The essay was an appreciation of Tennyson's 'Tis better to have loved and lost than never to have loved at all,' which Pearson later described as 'a triumph of imagination over experience'.

In September 1915 a combined allied force, including the Canadian medical corps, was sent to Salonica in Macedonia to assist Serbia, which was being overrun by Austrian, German, and Bulgarian forces. There Lester Pearson's last illusions of the adventure and romance of war were destroyed. The medical corps set up its tents in fields that were turned to mud by rain and sleet. Each day the men tended new casualties brought in on wagons pulled by horses; the dead and dying were moved to one side and the medical officer would go around with his lantern, doing what he could to ease the soldiers' pain. When the fighting lulled in November, the Macedonian plain was struck by a fierce blizzard that left the wounded outnumbered in the medical tents by the frostbitten and the sick. By 1916 the front had been stabilized and both sides settled down in their trenches in a stalemate that lasted for many long months. Pearson was now working in the quartermaster store, having been judged unsuitable for duty in an operating tent when he fainted at the sight of the first incision. Although he had made a number of good friends, he was becoming increasingly bored and decided to try for a commission in the Canadian infantry. After applying unsuccessfully through the proper channels, he wrote his father for assistance. Although his parents

'Mike' Pearson in army uniform (second from right).

Playing for the Oxford team at Murren, Switzerland, 1921.

did not like the thought of his receiving a commission that would likely lead him to the front, his father contacted the Minister of the Militia, Sam Hughes, whom he knew, and Pearson was sent to Oxford, England, for training. There he met both his brothers and spent an enjoyable four months in the spring of 1917. Although he did not distinguish himself in military tactics or musketry, he won first prize for throwing a cricket ball during a batallion sports day.

Having reached the rank of lieutenant, Pearson was expecting to go to the front when the Allied Command, faced with an alarming loss of pilots, appealed for volunteers for the Royal Flying Corps. Pearson, who had developed a fascination for flying while in Macedonia, applied at once and was accepted. The need for pilots was so great that he was given a scant three-weeks of ground training before being sent to the outskirts of London where, after only one hour and forty minutes of instruction, he was sent up on his own. Getting the plane into the air proved to be no problem, but he was less sure about his ability to land. He kept the plane in flight until he realized he might soon run out of gas, then he brought it down for a bumpy but successful landing. It was during this period that he received something that would prove to be far longer-lasting than his flying ability: a new name. Upon his transfer to the Royal Flying Corps a senior officer looked him over and said: 'Lester—that's not a very belligerent name for a man who wants to be a fighter pilot. We'll call you Mike.' The name stuck, although those who had known him before 1917 continued to call him Lester.

Despite his high hopes, Mike Pearson never did see action as a fighter pilot. While banking in preparation for landing during another training flight, his engine stalled and the plane crashed. Pearson was not badly injured, but he was sufficiently shaken up to be given a few days off to recuperate. During this period of convalescence he decided to relieve his boredom by taking a bus into London for a night on the town. After a pleasant supper with some friends, an air-raid warning was announced and Pearson hopped on a bus to return to his base. They had not gone far before a bomb exploded less than half-a-mile away; the bus driver decided to go no further before an all-clear was sounded. Pearson stepped down from the bus and walked behind it to cross the road when he was suddenly struck by another bus, whose lights were off because of the air raid and whose driver had therefore not been able to see him. Pearson, knocked unconscious, suffered far more serious injuries than he had during the crash of his plane. After several weeks in hospital and a convalescent home, he was sent back to Canada. For him the war was over.

By this time, the fall of 1917, Pearson and others of his generation had come to realize the full horror of war. The war of attrition, marked by occasional forays, massive slaughters, and hasty retreats, had lost all its glamour and was seen to be nothing but a gruesome stupidity. Almost everyone, Pearson included, lost close friends in action. The question that they soon asked themselves was, 'Why?' A whole generation of young Canadians returned from Europe with a determination never again to become involved in such a massive slaughter. During his period of convalescence in London Pearson began to reflect for the first time on the deeper significance of war. It left a lasting impression on him, and caused him later in life to be a tireless crusader for peace. Reflecting on his war experiences later, Pearson remarked: 'I got hurt before I got a chance to get killed—that's about what it amounts to . . . I never expected to come back from that war. You got to a point after a few years overseas when you just went on until you were killed, like all your friends were being killed. The only thing that would save you from being killed was being wounded, and getting out of it.'

By the spring of 1918 Mike Pearson was back in Toronto where, after serving as an instructor in aerial navigation, he resumed his studies at the University of Toronto in January 1919. He had been given his third year because of his overseas service, a standard practice, and now entered the fourth year of his honours history course, which was already half over. His study habits returned quickly and he caught up on his missed work sufficiently well to be granted his Bachelor of Arts degree, with honours, on June 5, 1919. Like many graduates, he was then faced with the puzzling question of what to do next. He toyed with the idea of law school until he began reading a book on contract law ('the dullest book which I had ever read'); this quickly discouraged him from pursuing a legal career. After an enjoyable summer in Guelph, where he played semi-professional baseball to pass the time and earn some money, he decided to join the world of business. He applied for a job with the Armour Leather Company in Chicago, of which his uncle was president, and was told to report to the company's Canadian subsidiary, the Fowler Packing Company in Hamilton. There he was given the job of stuffing sausages into containers, which was made only barely endurable by the existence in Hamilton of a good hockey team, on which Pearson was able to work out his frustrations. He was transferred to the Chicago office as a clerk in the spring but had realized by this time that, even though he was beginning to move up the ladder, he had no real wish to remain in business. By the winter of 1921 he became aware for the first time of what he really wanted to do: finish his education and then teach history at a university.

At first he hesitated to tell his uncle that the meat-packing industry held little appeal for him. When he finally summoned the courage, he was relieved by his uncle's reaction. 'Go right ahead,' he told Mike. 'Don't worry about any business prospects you feel you may have lost. Try to find the kind of work you enjoy doing. Not too many people are able to get that satisfaction. Find out what you want to do and stick to it. You may be surprised at where it will lead you.' Pearson remembered the advice, which he considered among the most important he ever received. (His brief period with Armour and Company came to the fore later in life when the Russians charged that he had once worked for an 'armaments company'.)

Pearson's dream was to go to Oxford, which had fascinated him when he saw it during the war, although he expected that he would have to stay in Canada to continue his studies because of financial considerations. Nevertheless he decided to apply for a Vincent Massey scholarship to Oxford, which, because of his good marks, he received. Next followed two years at St John's College, Oxford, that he later recalled as the happiest of his life. He enjoyed his studies in modern history and began to mature intellectually. Above all there was sports. He played on the lacrosse team, which achieved such success that it was sent on a month-long tour of American universities during the 1922 Easter vacation. Oxford's hockey team, dominated by Canadians, destroyed almost all opposition. One game against Cambridge, which had no Canadian Rhodes scholars, was called at the end of the second period with Oxford leading 27-0. During the Christmas holidays the team toured Swiss winter resorts, winning easily, and Pearson even played for the Swiss national team in the European championships since eligibility rules were very loose. This experience later entitled him to quip that he was the only Prime Minister in the world who had represented Switzerland in ice-hockey. Pearson also played tennis with many Canadian friends at Oxford, including one from Alberta, Roland Michener, who was to become Canada's third native-born Governor General.

Near the end of his second year at Oxford, Pearson was approached by the head of the history department at the University of Toronto, G. M. Wrong, on one of his visits to Oxford. He told Pearson that there was an opening in the history department and that, since his record was good, he would be offered a job if he received a 'first' in his exams. Pearson's oral exam was uneventful; he took it with another student, the captain of the college rowing team, and recalled that the professors spent fifty-five of the sixty minutes discussing rowing with the captain and had time to ask him only one question. In his written exams he made a 'second class' but was close enough to a first to persuade Professor Wrong to renew his offer. By the autumn of 1923, at the age of twenty-six, he was a lecturer in modern history at the University of Toronto and a don at one of the university residences, which entitled him to a comfortable – free – apartment. For the first time in his life he felt financially secure, convinced that he had found his chosen field.

Life as a history lecturer at the University of Toronto was comfortable and interesting. In addition to teaching his courses (which included European history from 1815 to 1914, the development of the British Commonwealth, British constitutional history, England under the Stuarts, and the

The Pearsons' wedding picture, August 22, 1925.

Reformation and the Renaissance), he coached the Victoria College football team to the interfaculty championship in his first year, and in his second he coached the university football and hockey teams. In the classroom his friendly and informal manner and quick wit made him popular and effective, and he was soon promoted to assistant professor. 'I liked teaching,' Pearson recalled many years later, 'and I think I was reasonably successful as a teacher. I wasn't a great scholar but I think I was a good teacher. I wasn't interested in the kind of scholarly research that is required now to get ahead in the academic profession.'

The degree of affection for Professor Pearson varied among his students. One of them was Maryon Elspeth Moody, the daughter of a Winnipeg physician, who in a letter to a friend remarked on 'a very interesting young history professor named Mike Pearson'. In his memoirs Pearson wrote that, among the girls in his European history class, 'one pretty dark-haired girl with a clear and enquiring mind (which, as a professor, was what I was supposed to be solely concerned with) was by far the most attractive of the eight . . . In March 1924, with final examinations approaching, Maryon Moody decided that, while it might not be necessary, an easy way to ensure that she would get her degree was to become engaged to her teacher. It worked.' They were married in Winnipeg on August 22, 1925. The Pearsons moved into a small flat not far from the University of Toronto, where they lived comfortably, though not luxuriously, on his modest professor's salary. From the outset Mrs Pearson took over the running of the household. She managed the budget, paid the bills, chose her husband's suits, and in later years, when they were able to afford this luxury, bought the family car. Pearson gladly left these tasks in her capable hands, especially when the demands of his work left him little time to think of such matters. With her candid frankness that Mike's political colleagues later frequently found embarrassing, she provided Pearson with a happy and rewarding family life.

In the summer of 1926 the Pearsons went to Ottawa to do research in the National Archives. Pearson had begun to think of getting a Ph.D. to further his academic career, or at least of writing a book. The head of the history department suggested that a history of Canada's United Empire Loyalists might make a good project and this appealed to Pearson on the grounds that Canadian history was sadly neglected at most Canadian universities. The Pearsons spent the summer busily sifting through the records of the Archives. In the evenings they hiked along the lakes and through the Gatineau hills overlooking Ottawa to the north, just across the Ottawa River in Québec. Other evenings Pearson spent in the gallery of the House of Commons, sensing for the first time the excitement of political and parliamentary life and the privilege of seeing well-known political figures.

The winter of 1927 was highlighted by the birth of the first of their two children, Geoffrey. During this same winter Pearson heard that examinations were to be conducted by the Civil Service Commission for first and third secretaries in the newly formed Department of External Affairs. He received a letter from Dr O. D. Skelton, the man chosen by Prime Minister King to organize the new department, whom he had met during his summer of research in Ottawa. Skelton suggested that Pearson might like to take the exam. Pearson felt no particular desire to leave university life, but decided, when the application forms were sent to him in the spring, to write the five-part examination and see what happened. If he were not accepted, it would be no great loss; on the other hand if he were successful, he would decide then what he wanted to do.

When the Civil Service Commission eventually assembled a list of prospective candidates, Skelton decided to seek the views of Vincent Massey, who was then Canadian minister to Washington but who had met several of the candidates while teaching history at the University of Toronto. Part of Massey's reply to him read: 'I am interested in what you say about Pearson's prospects. I saw something of him when he first came back from Oxford. My only criticism of him in connection with his possible appointment is that there is something curiously loose-jointed and sloppy about his mental makeup which, as a matter of fact, is reflected in some measure in his physical bearing. It is possible, however, that his other qualities offset this defect.' Two days later Dr Skelton wrote back: 'I have just had an interview with Pearson. You have exactly hit the nail on the head. There is something curiously loose jointed in his physical bearing and perhaps to a lesser extent in his mental makeup. At the same time he has a very distinct capacity and attractive personal qualifications. . . . ' Despite these initial reservations, Pearson was not only selected as a foreign-service officer but led the list of sixty candidates (although it occurred to him that his veteran's preference might have been responsible for his first-place showing). When the telegram of acceptance arrived, Pearson had just undergone an eye test and his pupils were still dilated from the eye-drops. Unable to focus and read the message, he walked over to the library and asked one of the librarians to read him the telegram. It read: 'Civil Service Commission report you first in competition for First Secretary post. Can you report at Department Monday.'

Now he had a decision to make. He had recently been promoted to assistant professor and director of athletics at almost double his original salary: he was well on the road to a successful university career. On the other hand the External Affairs position, with the opportunity to get into a fledgling department at a high level, was very tempting. Maryon Pearson felt that if he stayed at Toronto his job as director of athletics would gradually supersede his teaching—there would not be time for both. She was not enthusiastic about the prospect of being married to a sports director and her views, as usual, carried great weight. Pearson decided to accept the new position.

Pearson's decision to enter the Department of External Affairs was very typical of his approach to life. He did not have any one main goal that he wished to achieve, nor was there any particular position to which he aspired. He would have been perfectly content to stay at the University of Toronto had this new opportunity not presented itself, just as in the years that followed he would have been happy to remain in the civil service rather than enter politics. His formula for life, inherited from his father, was that 'to deserve success is more important than to achieve it.' One of the qualities that others found most attractive in Pearson was his apparent lack of self-seeking ambition. But from his parents he had also learned that every individual had the responsibility to improve the world in which he lived. Therefore, as each new opportunity presented itself during his life, Pearson was pushed forward by the feeling, sometimes subconscious, that he had an obligation to accept new challenges. There would be numerous times in Pearson's career when an unexpected opportunity aroused in him an instinct to accept it.

2

Diplomat

Canada in the 1920s was a far different country from the one that had entered the First World War. There was a new awareness of national achievement and a feeling among its citizens of being Canadian, not British. This growth of national consciousness resulted from Canada's monumental contribution to the winning of the war. Out of 619,636 Canadians who had served in the army, 51,748 had been killed. Canadians had fought gallantly in many of the war's major battles and had gained a reputation for great courage and efficiency. The economy had been harnessed to the war effort and both industrial and agricultural production had been increased to meet the allies' demands. There was more talk of national character in literature and the arts and a concrete manifestation of the new feeling of identity in paintings of the Canadian landscape by the artists who became known collectively as the 'Group of Seven'.

To many Canadians the fact that the country's foreign policy was controlled by Great Britain was no longer satisfactory. Although Canada was autonomous in its domestic affairs in 1914, it had no diplomatic relations with other countries, no treaty-making power, and was seen by the outside world as a British colony. Canada's foreign policy was made in London, and when Great Britain went to war against Germany, Canada was automatically involved. After the war this dependence on England was inconsistent with the growing feeling of nationalism in Canada. The government of Prime Minister Robert Borden demanded the right to participate in the signing of the peace treaties ending the war, rather than having Britain sign on behalf of Canada and the other Dominions. The next step was for Canada to build up its own diplomatic service, which had been limited before the war to maintaining trade commissioners and immigration agents in a few countries, including Britain and France. Authority for this was provided by the Balfour Declaration of 1926, drawn up at the imperial conference of Dominion heads of government in London, which stated that Great Britain and the Dominions were 'autonomous communities within the British Empire, equal in status, and in no way subordinate one to another in any aspect of their domestic or external affairs'.

In 1925 the Department of External Affairs consisted of three officers working out of the Prime Minister's office, since Canada had few international activities to worry about. After the Balfour Declaration, however, Prime Minister Mackenzie King realized the need to expand the diplomatic service. After all, as one commentator observed, control over one's own foreign affairs, without satisfactory machinery to exercise that control, 'would be as useless as a licence to drive without a motor car'. The result was a recruiting drive in 1927, which brought Lester Pearson into the department. Dr O. D. Skelton, the department's under-secretary, wanted to build up 'a small staff of young men, well educated and carefully selected', and by the end of 1930 the department had grown in size to eighteen officers—though this was a paltry number compared with the staffs in other government departments even in those days. Pearson was clearly in the fortunate position of moving into a new department at a very high level. Canada's first foreign mission was opened in 1927 in Washington, and the high commission in London, already in existence, soon received diplomatic status. With the opening in 1928 of legations in Paris and Tokyo, Canada was represented in four foreign countries. The fledgling Department of External Affairs had begun to grow.

As first secretary in what was considered the 'élite' department of government, Pearson became involved in a social life that was considerably more elaborate than any he had previously known. The Pearsons were invited to ministerial and diplomatic receptions, and the strictly raised son of a Methodist minister had to learn how to make a cocktail when he entertained. The increased salary enabled the Pearsons to buy their first car, a second-hand Ford, and to move from their apartment into a house in 1929 when the arrival of their second child, Patricia, made the flat too small. Ottawa proved to be a comfortable and pleasant city in which to live. It lacked the cultural attractions of major world capitals, but it offered a multitude of outdoor charms, including rivers, parks, a canal, and, just across the Ottawa River, the Gatineau hills of Québec. For exercise Pearson played tennis in the summer and squash in the winter.

The Department of External Affairs was quartered in the oldest building on Parliament Hill, the East Block, a stately turreted edifice in which the Prime Minister's office was also located. It was the first government building constructed in Ottawa after Confederation, and Pearson found himself sharing an inelegant room in the attic with two other new officers. His assignments were many and varied. Among his first were the scanning of British treaties to see how many were

Canadian delegation to the Disarmament Conference, London, Eng., 1930: Walter Hose, J. L. Ralston, Pearson, H. W. Brown.

applicable to Canada and the drawing up of a brief on Canada's position at a League of Nations conference. In 1929 he was even sent to Washington to take charge of the Canadian legation there for the summer. It was not really a promotion, however; it was customary for embassies in Washington to send their staff to the seaside to escape the humid heat of the city during the summer, and to leave a junior officer to deal with any minor matters that might arise. Nevertheless it was a sign of the Department's confidence in Pearson that he was given the assignment. In 1930 he was sent to London to advise the Canadian delegation to the London Naval Conference, one in a series of unsuccessful attempts at disarmament during the period between the two world wars. Mrs Pearson went with him and, by careful budgeting and by ordering one meal for two people, they were able to manage on a modest expense allowance.

In the 1930s Pearson was involved in several projects that had little if anything to do with international relations. The Department of External Affairs was in the unique position of having as its minister the Prime Minister himself, with the result that successive prime ministers often turned to it for advice and assistance on questions of internal as well as external policy. This was particularly true of Prime Minister Bennett, who defeated Mackenzie King in the election of 1930. He was far less enthusiastic than King had been about developing an independent foreign service and, besides, the economic problems of the great Depression that was just beginning forced him to concentrate his attention on domestic matters. During Bennett's five years as Prime Minister, Pearson frequently worked out of his office and travelled with him. He also served on two Royal Commissions, one dealing with the study of trading in grain futures and the other with price spreads between producers and consumers. Through this work Pearson acquired a basic knowledge of Canadian social and economic conditions that was to prove useful when he entered politics. He also impressed the commissioners with his ability to write clear and concise resumés of arguments, highlighting important points and drawing logical conclusions, and with his capacity for hard work. In recognition of his contribution in organizing the Price Spreads Commission and in supervising the preparation of its impressive report, the Prime Minister included Pearson in a list of names that he planned to submit for the King's annual honours list. When Pearson learned of the proposed tribute he urged Mr Bennett to reconsider, for he knew that Dr Skelton, his deputy minister, would not be pleased to see one of his officers publicly decorated for performing duties that were expected of him. Pearson suggested that, if the Prime Minister was determined to reward him, a more appropriate way might be to give him a promotion. 'Mr Prime Minister,' he said, 'I would settle for twenty-five dollars more a week. I can't raise a family on an OBE.' Bennett, not one to be deterred, replied that if Pearson made him change his list once again, not only would he not get an Order of the British Empire but he would never get a promotion as long as he was Prime Minister. Pearson said no more but in due course received both the OBE and a reclassification in grade.

In the mid-1930s Pearson represented Canada at various international conferences in Geneva, including sessions of the League of Nations. The League, a preliminary but much smaller version of the United Nations, had been created after the First World War to deter aggression by ensuring that any attack on a member-state would bring all other member-states to its defence. In other words, no country would risk attacking another if it knew that all the other countries of the League of Nations would join forces against it. This was the system of 'collective security' that seemed to be the world's only chance of avoiding another world war.

By 1935 the League was in serious trouble. It had taken no action against the Japanese invasion of Manchuria in 1931, and two years later Germany, now led by Adolf Hitler, withdrew its membership. In 1935 Mussolini's Italy invaded Ethiopia. This was an act of aggression and it was clear to all that if the League of Nations did nothing, there could be no hope for an effective system of collective security. Events at first looked promising, particularly when Great Britain announced that it would support resistance to acts of aggression. On the morning of the day on which the Assembly was scheduled to decide whether Italy had broken the rules of the League Covenant, the Canadian delegation received a telegram from Prime Minister Bennett in Ottawa instructing it not to vote on such an important issue since the Canadian Parliament had been dissolved and the country was in the midst of an election campaign. The Canadian delegation, led by G. Howard Ferguson, was astounded; there could be no doubt about Italy's guilt, and an abstention by Canada would be interpreted as a desire not to enforce the collective security provisions of the covenant. Ferguson decided that, rather than be put in the embarrassing position of having to abstain, he would simply not attend the Assembly meeting. 'We'll go and play golf,' he announced. Pearson, a secretary and adviser to the delegation, suggested that they try to telephone Mr Bennett and get their instructions changed. It was the first telephone call ever made from their Geneva office to Ottawa, but they eventually got through to the Prime Minister, who was on the campaign trail and took the call in the

stationmaster's office at Lindsay, Ont. While Pearson listened, at Ferguson's request, on another phone, Bennett
agreed that the Canadian delegation should go ahead and
vote the way it felt best.

Eventually the League drew up proposals for sanctions that
should be applied against Italy. Pearson later recalled that he
had never been so emotional about anything in international
relations as when the decision was taken to apply sanctions
against an aggressor under the League Covenant. There was
hope that peace could be preserved. However, he did not
then know that his own government would soon let him
down. The 1935 election resulted in the defeat of Bennett
and the re-election of Mackenzie King, who was afraid of
accepting commitments in Europe that might involve Canada
in another war. Like many other Canadians and Europeans,
he thought that the rise of totalitarian régimes in Germany
and Italy was nothing to be afraid of, that the world was
simply witnessing a rebirth of the traditional rivalries of
European powers. Above all, he felt that Canada should
concentrate on its own problems and let Europe look after
itself. The new head of the Canadian delegation, Dr Riddell,
did not, however, receive any precise instructions from
Ottawa and therefore pressed in the Assembly to make the
economic sanctions against Italy more effective. He argued
that petroleum, iron, and steel should be added to the list of
goods that could not be traded with Italy. Prime Minister
King was appalled, feeling that such an action risked antagonizing Italy and would lead to war. Pearson and others
argued to the contrary—that tough sanctions were needed to
prevent war and that without them any country would feel
free to attack another. The Prime Minister repudiated Riddell's initiative, and the unfortunate delegate soon found him-

self in Chile engaged in other duties. Canada was not alone in its cautious attitude, however. Both Britain and France began to fear that harsh sanctions would do more harm than good and backed away from their earlier support of the idea. Ethiopia was left to be overrun by Italy. Pearson later pointed to this failure as the turning-point that led to the Second World War. If all countries had stood up to Italy, he said in a 1942 speech, Hitler's Germany would never have dared pursue its aggressive policies.

After Riddell's departure, Pearson replaced him as head of the Canadian delegation to the League even though, because of his government's policy, he could not do or say what he wanted. Mackenzie King's unwillingness to accept international commitments had to be taken into consideration at other conferences that Pearson attended during this period. Describing an international sugar conference at which he represented Canada, Pearson wrote in his diary: 'Of course no one here has any idea whatever as to what the Canadian attitude toward this conference is, or even if there is a Canadian attitude. But I was reluctant to say that, so I chatted amiably for fifteen minutes . . . of course I kept carefully away from the sugar conference itself because I knew nothing about it; I kept even more carefully away from Canadian policy.'

Despite the frustrations, it was still an exciting era for diplomats. Pearson became acquainted with many major international figures. He played tennis with Anthony Eden, a British delegate who was to become Foreign Secretary and eventually Prime Minister, and even joined a Swiss hockey team that played during weekends—much to the surprise of many of his diplomatic colleagues. He never tired of poking fun at the pretensions of some of his associates, who, he felt, took themselves far too seriously. A Canadian trade official who went up to Pearson's room in the Hôtel de la Paix in Geneva described their meeting. Greeting him at the door, Pearson whispered 'Shhh,' locked the door, and proceeded to look in the cupboards, under the beds, and behind the curtains before breathing a sigh of relief. 'Everything's all right,' he said, explaining that if one did not whisper, one was considered to be of no importance, to have no secrets, and therefore to be of no significance. 'Thus,' he told his friend, 'if you see two diplomats buttonholing each other and earnestly whispering to each other, they are probably asking each other what they had for lunch.'

With the League of Nations in the throes of death, there remained little work to do in Geneva and Pearson was sent to Canada House in London. From the outset the entire family fell in love with England. They found a house in Hampstead, with a girls' school and a boys' school nearby. Pearson, who disliked all large cities, soon considered London 'the only great city in the world fit to live in', and he and his family spent many happy days exploring it. In the course of time they also explored England and Scotland from Land's End to John o'Groats. The United Kingdom, Pearson nostalgically told a farewell dinner upon his departure in 1941, represents 'the furthest and finest stage mankind has yet reached in political and social development.' However, Pearson was not (as one of his contemporaries in the British foreign service, Lord Garner, put it) a 'starry-eyed admirer' of the country, for 'He could easily be enraged with British arrogance, stuffiness, snobbery, condescension.' Pearson himself liked to joke that he never felt so pro-British as when he was in Washington, or so pro-American as when he was in London.

At Canada House Pearson served under two senior diplomats who were destined to become Canada's first two
native-born Governors General, Vincent Massey and
Georges Vanier. Massey, the High Commissioner, had close
personal contacts with artists, aristocrats, and indeed with the
Royal Family. His connections with the social and governmental Establishment of England bothered Mackenzie King,
who was always suspicious of Downing Street and strongly
favoured Canada's keeping its distance from British imperial
politics. Vanier was the next in rank to the High Commissioner. After him came Pearson. (It was an indication of
Pearson's ability—but even more of the small size of Canada's foreign service—that he should have occupied such a
senior position after less than ten years in the department.)
Together they made an impressive and efficient team. In his
memoirs Vincent Massey wrote: 'When I took up my post in
London in 1935, I was lucky to find as the two senior
members of the staff Georges Vanier and L. B. Pearson—
able colleagues and warm friends, both of them. No chief
could have been more grateful than I was for what they did.'

Pearson's duties were, as usual, varied. They involved such
things as helping Canadians get in touch with relatives fighting in the Spanish civil war, assisting Europeans wishing to
immigrate to Canada, and sending dispatches back to Ottawa
on the political situation in Britain. For this latter task he
depended for information on his many contacts in the British
government, which he cultivated with care, like any good
diplomat, sometimes at Whitehall, sometimes at lunch, sometimes at an official dinner in the evening. His diplomatic
rank also entitled him to be present at England's most important social event of 1937, the coronation of King George VI.
With the grand title of 'Gold Stick in Waiting', Pearson was

to serve as an usher. He dressed for the ceremony in knee breeches, silk stockings, buckled shoes, black cutaway coat, cocked hat, and sword—a rented costume extemporized by Moss Brothers. When he arrived at Westminster Abbey at 4:30 on the morning of the coronation, he discovered that his post of duty was behind a pillar and so far from the altar that he would be able to see nothing of the actual coronation. After his section had been filled, he and a South African diplomat decided to look for a better spot. Discovering a door in a tower, they climbed a long spiralling staircase and found an opening just large enough to look through; below them was the main transept of the Abbey and a perfect view of the altar. Pearson watched the crowning of the King and Queen from one of the best vantage spots in the Abbey.

Other duties were more serious. Prime Minister King was increasingly worried that Canada's new-found external independence would be compromised if it became too closely involved with British policy. Pearson and his colleagues found themselves having to defend their meetings with British officials to Mr King, who felt that the officials of Canada House were becoming too influenced by the British government. Pearson and Massey, on the other hand, believed that relations between the two countries should be warm, especially as the threat of war brought the likelihood that the two countries would again be involved in a common struggle. Of their commitment to Canadian independence, however, there could be no doubt. In many speeches that he delivered in England, Pearson expressed the conviction that Canada would remain fully independent, although he recognized that in the future it was the United States and not Britain against which Canada would have to assert its separate identity.

The most serious problem of all, of course, was the

approaching war. Pearson, like many of his contemporaries, had originally been skeptical that Hitler's Germany harboured any aggressive intentions. It was only in retrospect that he came to realize the full significance of the failure of the League of Nations to impose effective sanctions against Italy in 1935. Hitler, he thought at the time, was merely attempting to remove the injustices that Germany had suffered in the Treaty of Versailles of 1919 when he ordered the German army to occupy the Rhineland in 1935. With the occupation of Austria in 1938, Pearson began to change his views. Unlike the Rhineland, Austria was not German land that had been taken away in 1919. Hitler's true nature was also impressed upon him by Winston Churchill, whom Pearson heard speak on the dangers of Nazism at a London club. In his analysis of the situation for Ottawa, Pearson wrote: 'Even if you accept the view that the boa constrictor, as Churchill picturesquely put it, will now uncoil and rest while the process of digestion goes on, events in Austria show that this process is pretty fast in our mechanical age. Furthermore, I simply cannot feel that this particular boa constrictor's appetite is going to be satisfied by the most recent sheep.' Mackenzie King and his top advisers in Ottawa, however, remained unconvinced of Hitler's aggressive intentions. They reasoned that by a policy of appeasement—not objecting to the occupation of Austria and, later, Czechoslovakia—Hitler's appetite would be satiated and he would not want any more territory. The government believed that conciliation of Germany, not massive rearmament, was the best policy, despite the gloomily realistic reports coming to it from Canada House.

In the summer of 1939 the Pearsons returned to Canada on home leave for a vacation on the shores of Lac du Bonnet

in Manitoba. Then one day Pearson saw a newspaper head-
line that read: 'Nazis Threaten Danzig and the Polish Corridor'. Knowing that war was certain if the Germans invaded
Poland, he decided he should return to London immediately
to look after matters there. Upon his arrival back in Ottawa
from Manitoba, Pearson was invited by Mackenzie King to
dine with him at his summer home at Kingsmere. The Prime
Minister told Pearson not to worry, that this latest crisis
would soon be resolved, and that he was convinced Hitler did
not want a general war. He urged him to rejoin his family
and finish his home leave. Pearson, however, was firm in his
decision to return to London and King said he could do as
he wished. By this time Pearson was convinced that war was
only days away and that he would be too late if he returned
by ship. He convinced the department to let him fly and
made the trip on Pan American Airways, which had begun
its first transatlantic flights only that summer.

Pearson arrived in London less than a week before the
British declaration of war on September 3. (Canada's own
declaration of war was made by a Cabinet order-in-council
passed on September 10.) Minutes after the war had officially
begun, air-raid sirens sounded and the staff of Canada House
proceeded dutifully downstairs into the furnace room, which
had been set up as an emergency bomb shelter. Their orders
were to stay there until they received word from Whitehall,
through a special telephone, that the danger was over. Time
passed, the shelter became hotter and hotter, but still the
phone did not ring. Finally Pearson persuaded the High
Commissioner to let him go upstairs and find out what was
happening. Massey agreed and Pearson climbed slowly up to
the ground floor, where he peeked carefully through a win-
dow. To his amazement he saw nothing but the normal sights

of Trafalgar Square. It had been a false alarm and nobody had thought to tell the staff of Canada House.

By this time Pearson was second-in-command at Canada House (Vanier had been appointed ambassador to France in January) and he was swamped with work. He had to look after arrangements for a possible evacuation of Canada House and its transfer to the countryside in the event that German attacks on London became too severe; help Canadian tourists return home; and trace Canadian citizens still on the continent. Another time-consuming task was dealing with the many long telegrams that Prime Minister King delighted in sending to Canada House. On one occasion, in a cable marked 'Secret and Most Urgent', King asked for some of the stones from the British House of Commons, which had been damaged by a German air raid. He wanted them for the ruins he enjoyed erecting at Kingsmere. Pearson feared that the British government, preoccupied with the problems of war and fighting for the very survival of the country, would not welcome a request to ship some stones to Canada. Nevertheless he dutifully submitted the request and it was not long before the stones were on their way to Kingsmere.

The Prime Minister also liked to send telegrams direct to the British Prime Minister rather than through the Canadian High Commission, as was customary. The result was that Pearson and Massey often did not know about a Canadian position, as expressed by Mr King, until they were told of it by the British. What was worse, the British government was beginning to become annoyed by Mr King's 'cable verbosity', since it had to decode the Canadian Prime Minister's lengthy messages, many of which had little if anything to do with the war effort and could have been sent in ordinary code. Pearson was asked by British officials whether he might somehow

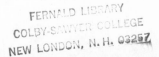

be able to encourage Mr King to reduce the number and length of his telegrams. Pearson replied that he feared his diplomatic talents were not equal to the task of drafting a message to the Prime Minister of Canada telling him, without offending him, not to be so verbose.

Only rarely during this time was Pearson or even Massey closely involved in major questions of military policy or strategy. For the most part the British government preferred to deal with such questions with a minimum of consultation; when Canada *was* involved, the discussions usually took place at a high political level, often between prime ministers. One exception involved the early negotiations for the creation of the Commonwealth Air Training Programme. Britain, knowing that more pilots would be needed for the war effort, proposed that Canada should be the centre for the training of pilots from all countries of the Commonwealth. The negotiations were prolonged and difficult, for Canada felt that the original British proposals would impose too great a financial burden and wanted to ensure that Canadian airmen who were trained in the program would be placed in Canadian formations and not merged with the Royal Air Force.

One reason that discussions between Britain and Canada were often prolonged during this period was that few people realized the seriousness of the military situation. The fighting in Poland, which had provoked Britain's entry into the war, had ended, and for several months there were no major military engagements. Pearson was preoccupied with such administrative matters as the arrival in Britain of the first Canadian troops. One of his responsibilities was to act as liaison between Canadian military authorities and British civil officials. 'This included,' he wrote later, 'putting blunt Canadian military language into acceptable officialese designed to make a favourable impression at Whitehall when we wanted something done. It also meant interpreting austere Whitehall language in plainer terms more familiar to our own military authorities. I had been in the diplomatic service long enough to claim some skill in what I used to call quintuplet diplomatic communications, those requiring at least five copies. Indeed, I once agreed with a desk-bound soldier friend of mine at Canadian Military Headquarters that if we lost the war it would not be due to the German army but to the exhaustion of the supply of allied carbon paper.'

In the spring of 1940, any illusions that might have been held about the war's being over quickly were shattered. In a massive lightning assault, German forces overran Belgium, Holland, and France. The success of this blitzkrieg demonstrated the relative weakness of the countries of Western Europe in the face of Hitler's revitalized Germany. By autumn, German bombers were conducting regular attacks on London itself and there was a danger that the Royal Air Force would not be able to match the Luftwaffe. The collapse of the countries of Western Europe—especially France —and the prospect that even Britain might soon face invasion suddenly prompted a high degree of co-operation when the allies negotiated among themselves.

One day, in September 1940, several officials of Canada House, including Vanier and Pearson, toured areas in the east end of London that had recently been bombed. 'It was a heart-breaking experience,' Vanier later wrote. 'The worst place was in East Ham where we saw street after street of little houses—either burnt or shattered by blast.' On another occasion Pearson was speaking at University College in Nottingham on the subject of Canada and the United States when a note was sent up to the chairman. He interrupted

Pearson to announce that an air-raid alert had been sounded; with the distinguished speaker's permission, those who wished to leave for home or an air-raid shelter should do so. Few chose to leave, however, and Pearson continued his address. A few moments later the chairman interrupted to read a second note, which said that enemy aircraft were overhead and bombs had begun to fall in another part of the city. This time almost half the audience left. Although the impact of his remarks had been considerably diminished, Pearson doggedly continued until there was a sudden and final announcement that fire bombs were burning in the neighbouring building. This was too much for even the heroic English audience that was left and the meeting dissolved in confusion. Pearson never ceased to be impressed by the stoic manner with which the English carried on their daily activities in spite of the constant threat of bombing, which destroyed much of the city of London. As he was teeing off one Sunday morning during his weekly golf game, his caddy advised him to slice a little more than usual since there was an unexploded bomb in the middle of the fairway. He told Pearson there was no danger, however; a red flag had been placed over it to identify it as a 'hazard'.

Pearson might well have spent the rest of the war in London had it not been for the sudden death in 1941 of Dr Skelton, the department's under-secretary. He was succeeded by Norman Robertson, who had worked closely with Skelton and King in Ottawa. On learning of Skelton's death, Pearson at first hoped that he would be appointed his successor, since he was the only senior officer who had served both overseas and in Ottawa. He was not chosen, but his disappointment was tempered by the fact that he and Robertson were close friends. One of Robertson's first acts was to ask Pearson to return to Ottawa as his chief assistant and Pearson accepted the offer. He was anxious to rejoin his family, which had been in Ottawa since the fall of France. Massey, however, was very sorry to see him go. 'He possessed all the qualities essential to the difficult job he had been doing: initiative, a first-rate mind, imagination, great tact, and the human characteristics that have always made him a delightful companion.'

Pearson returned to an Ottawa buzzing with gossip that he resented Robertson's appointment. He was more popular than Robertson and seniority was also in his favour. Since he was scheduled to speak to a luncheon club, Pearson used the opportunity to put an end to the gossip. 'I want it known right now,' he said, 'that I think Norman Robertson's appointment was an excellent one and that I will be glad to work with him. If anyone can take Dr Skelton's place, he is the man.'

Pearson's responsibilities in Ottawa were even greater than they had been in London. He was now second-in-command not just of a High Commission but of the whole department. He worked on interdepartmental committees involved in the preparation of Canada's position on various war matters and on co-ordinating Canadian activity with Great Britain and the United States. One of Canada's major new problems, he quickly learned, was how to preserve its independent position from the encroachments of the United States, which had entered the war after the Japanese attack on Pearl Harbor in December 1941. 'United States – Canadian relations,' Pearson wrote Massey early in 1942, 'present a very difficult problem indeed in present circumstances. We are finding out that our cherished status is more respected in Downing Street than in Washington, and there are very definite and discernible tendencies in the latter capital to consider us either as a part of the British Empire to be dealt with through a British Empire spokesman from the United Kingdom or as a North American colony.' Just as Pearson had found it necessary while in London to prevent the British government from taking Canada for granted, so he now saw it would be necessary to impress Canada's independent status upon the United States.

In addition, Pearson began to develop a personal association with Prime Minister King during this period. After talking with Pearson on his return from London, King wrote in his diary that they had had a 'very interesting conversation on the whole [war] situation. He spoke of the amazing calm of the [English] people and their determination . . . Reported his readiness to begin work at once . . . Very modest, unassuming. He's going to be valuable to Robertson.' The two never became close, for their views on Canada's proper international role differed too greatly, particularly when Pearson was urging a strong Canadian involvement in the United Nations after the war. Nevertheless, King admired Pearson's ability and his talents for getting along with people and did not hesitate to give him a great deal of responsibility.

1941 was a happy year for the Pearson family, now re-united once more. The small size of the department was conducive to informal social contacts and the Pearsons had many friends throughout the civil service. The Gatineau hills retained their charm and the family made frequent excursions there. Pearson played tennis and belonged to a fishing club. In the fall they decided to buy a house, feeling that they were destined to spend many years in Ottawa, where Pearson was now a very senior civil servant.

One of the hazards of a diplomat's life, however, is the

complete lack of certainty about how long he will stay in any one place. Just as Pearson was getting comfortably installed in Ottawa, the head of the Canadian Legation in Washington, Leighton McCarthy, asked King to send Pearson as his number-two man. The Prime Minister agreed and the Pearsons were on the move again. In Washington his title was counsellor; in 1944 McCarthy left and Pearson became head of the mission, which was officially designated an Embassy in 1945, with Pearson becoming Canada's first ambassador to the United States.

During his period in Washington, Pearson became one of the most popular foreign diplomats with American government officials and journalists alike. He made close friends in both circles. While Leighton McCarthy, a friend of President Roosevelt, occupied himself with liaison between the Legation and the White House, Pearson was left with almost everything else: administration and organization of the mission, contacts with the American State Department, political reporting to Ottawa, and endless rounds of meetings dealing with the planning and conduct of the war. An indication of Pearson's involvement in nearly all aspects of the mission's work was Leighton McCarthy's wry comment to a Canadian journalist: 'I don't mind Mike running the whole legation but I wish, sometimes, that he'd tell me what we're doing.'

One of Pearson's major concerns was to ensure that Canada's contribution to the war effort was not overlooked by the United States or Great Britain. Prior to the allied invasion of Italy, for example, Prime Minister King learned that 'for reasons of security' the communiqué to be released after the landings would refer only to forces of the U.S. and the U.K. He hastily telephoned Pearson and told him to convince President Roosevelt that Canada's troops should be mentioned in the communiqué. They were. On other occasions the Americans and British would prepare plans for some aspect of the war without consulting Canada. Pearson became adept at using his contacts among diplomats of both countries, as well as the press, to find out what was going on so that Canada could have a voice in determining the eventual policy. The U.S. and U.K. also established a variety of combined boards and committees to deal with such questions as the mobilization of industrial and agricultural resources, and Canada made strong representations when they dealt with an area in which Canada had specific interests. Pearson was not always successful in getting Canada represented on these bodies, but his efforts forced the two major powers at least to take into consideration the Canadian point of view. The Canadian journalist Blair Fraser described Pearson's actions in this way: 'his informality of manner, and his knack for cutting through just the right amount of red tape, go down particularly well with the Americans. So well, indeed, that he is able to function not only as the proverbial 'linch-pin' between the U.S. and Britain, but on occasion to be an indignant—and heeded—exponent of small-power rights to the U.S. and Britain.'

By 1943 much of Pearson's attention was being focused on a variety of international conferences designed to ensure that peace would be maintained after the end of the war, which the allies were clearly winning. He was chairman of the Interim Commission set up to prepare for a permanent international organization dealing with food and agriculture (the Food and Agriculture Organization was later established within the United Nations). He was the Canadian representative on a committee concerned with the relief and rehabilitation of territories that had been occupied during the war, which resulted in the creation of the United Nations Relief and Rehabilitation Administration. He participated actively in discussions among the allied countries that led to their recommendation that the Atomic Energy Commission be set up under the United Nations to work towards the control and peaceful use of atomic energy. In these and a variety of other ways Pearson was involved in the establishment of the United Nations Organization. He made Canada's views known informally while the United States, the United Kingdom, the U.S.S.R., and China were drawing up a pre-liminary UN Charter at Dumbarton Oaks in 1944. He was convinced that the Second World War had been caused because the League of Nations had not been able to enforce the principle of collective security and that this was an oppor-tunity to apply the lessons of the past. The Charter should, he argued with the Americans and the British, include provi-sions for the imposition of sanctions against great powers as well as little ones. 'What is the use of having teeth if you cannot use them?' he wrote to Ottawa. 'What the Dumbarton Oaks Charter needs in fact is a little dentistry.'

For some time Mackenzie King had been thinking of putting Pearson in charge of the Washington mission. When Vincent Massey returned to Ottawa in March 1944 he dined with the Prime Minister and recorded their conversation in his diary: 'I talked about my visit to Washington and the excellent job which Mike Pearson was doing . . . The P.M. agreed. He suggested that there would be a change of Ambassador before a great while and asked whether I thought Mike would be a good successor to McCarthy. I said I thought he would.' In due course Pearson was given the responsibility for his first foreign mission. The duties of a head-of-delegation, which were very time-consuming, included making contacts with anyone who could be expected to provide information that would assist Canada in dealing with the United States. Pearson was remarkably well suited to this task. Lord Garner observed that Pearson's form of diplomacy 'was a highly personal one and largely depended on the impact he was able to make as an individual.' In this area he had few peers. Comparing him with two of his External Affairs colleagues, Norman Robertson and Arnold Heeney, Lord Garner added: 'If Robertson was the man to conceive an idea and Heeney the one to put it into practical form, Pearson had the gift of putting it across. He possessed to a remarkable extent a combination of qualities which made him unsurpassed in any negotiation—he was highly articulate and persuasive, and had a sufficient measure of idealism to convince one of his sincerity, yet at the same time always revealed a deft lightness of touch.' A U.S. diplomat with whom he had many dealings, Dean Acheson, observed in his memoirs that 'Pearson's speeches are always gay and witty'—although this trait became less apparent when he left the world of diplomacy for that of politics.

For a professional diplomat, Washington was a stimulating post. Arnold Heeney, who became Canadian ambassador to the U.S. in 1953, has written that he very soon 'became obsessed by the feeling that whatever happened, in the White House, in the vast government departments and agencies, in Congress, in the press, on television, even at the endless dinners and receptions, might somehow affect my country's interests and influence the course of world events.' Pearson's advice to Heeney at that time on how to handle his new position indicates the many duties and concerns of an ambassador: maintain good contacts with the administration, spend relatively less time with colleagues in the diplomatic corps,

With William Lyon Mackenzie King at the Canadian Embassy in Washington, September 29, 1945.

Atomic Bomb Conference, Washington, November 1945. Seated are Prime Minister Clement Atlee, President Harry S. Truman, and Prime Minister Mackenzie King. Pearson, then Canadian Ambassador to Washington, is behind President Truman.

San Francisco Conference, April-June 1945. Meeting of Canadian delegates. From left to right around the table: C. S. Ritchie, P. E. Renaud, Elizabeth MacCallum, Lucien Morand, Escott M. Reid, Warwick F. Chipman, L. B. Pearson, J. H. King, Louis St-Laurent, W. L. Mackenzie King, Gordon Graydon, M. J.

get to know important Senators and Congressmen, cultivate the press, travel and speak as much as possible, and make use of well-chosen lunches and dinners rather than larger social affairs. Pearson described his own period as ambassador in this way: 'I was privileged to meet and talk with the powerful men of the allied world, all of whom appeared in Washington at one time or another while I was there, and most of whom were entertained at the Canadian Embassy. Naturally we sent reports to Ottawa about these visits and what we had learned from the visitors, in the hope, not always vain, that in Ottawa they would be read and might be useful.'

In April 1945 government leaders from around the world met in San Francisco to settle the final details of—and to found officially—the United Nations Organization. The Canadian delegation was led by Prime Minister King; Pearson was present as a senior adviser. Pearson described his arrival in San Francisco, in the company of delegates and advisers from other countries, in his memoirs: 'We were met at the docks by various welcoming committees, put in motor cars, and whisked at break-neck speed to our various hotels, with motorcycle cops rushing madly ahead, sirens screaming. To make it all more exciting, they took us up the wrong side of the road and against red lights. It was a rather fantastic and nerve-racking performance. We arrived at the St Francis Hotel pretty shaken.' Their treatment was an indication of the importance of the Conference. Although the Canadian delegation was not able to achieve all it had hoped for in the way of making the UN a sufficiently strong instrument of collective security to deter future wars, it won many tributes from other delegations for its contribution to the debates as well as to the important committee deliberations that hammered out the final shape of the UN Charter. Canada's contribution to the formation of an agency to deal with important non-political matters—the Economic and Social Council—was recognized by all. Pearson participated actively in these discussions until he was called back to Washington, before the signing of the Charter, to attend to other business.

Around this time there was some speculation that Lester Pearson might become the first Secretary-General of the UN. Edward Stettinius, the chief American delegate on the preparatory commission for the establishment of the organization, had suggested earlier to Mackenzie King that both Pearson and Norman Robertson were possible choices. King wrote in his diary: 'I said I agreed they were the best men we had. It would be a great loss to Canada to lose either of them ... Stettinius questioned me somewhat on Pearson's abilities as a scholar as well as diplomat ... I was able to speak in the highest terms of both.' Pearson himself would have welcomed the job. He felt it would give him an unequalled opportunity to work for the things that concerned him the most: international peace, security, and co-operation. However, the choice had to be agreed upon by the Big Four powers—the U.S., the U.K., the U.S.S.R., and China—since the UN Charter gave all members of the Security Council a veto. The Soviets eventually decided that Pearson was too closely associated with the U.S. to be entirely neutral —or to favour them—and vetoed his name. Pearson had not really expected to be selected, and so was not too disappointed. Mackenzie King, on the other hand, was delighted not to lose one of his top civil servants.

In 1946 Pearson's career changed direction once more when he found himself at the top of the Department of External Affairs. This switch was occasioned by Vincent Massey's request to be relieved of his job as Canadian High

Commissioner in London and his replacement at Canada House by Norman Robertson. Robertson's departure left vacant the position of Under-Secretary of State for External Affairs, the highest non-political position in the department. On the evening of August 3, Pearson was asked by Prime Minister King whether he would accept the under-secretary's job. Pearson was at first reluctant, for he was just getting accustomed to his work as ambassador in Washington and felt he needed at least one more year there to take advantage of the experience he had gained. As well, the Pearsons had sold their house in Ottawa in 1941, and Pearson did not relish the thought of having to go through the bother of buying another. Finally, he had come to appreciate the importance of having an expense account for entertaining people and developing contacts, which he would no longer possess if he were not living abroad. If he had to leave Washington, he would have preferred to go to London as High Commissioner. However, King had already promised this post to Norman Robertson. The Prime Minister told Pearson that the money for his official entertaining in Ottawa would be 'managed somehow', and Pearson acceded to the request to return to Ottawa.

It was apparent from the reaction to Pearson's departure from Washington that he had been highly thought of in both official and non-official circles in the American capital. One of the *New York Times'* leading writers, James Reston, summed up what had become obvious to the many people with whom Pearson had come into contact in Washington: 'His main rule was informality ... He won the respect, confidence, and affection of a remarkably wide range of persons in most phases of Washington life ... After the melancholy catalogue of events in the field of foreign affairs these last few

years, few serious officials have been able to work incessantly
in the problem of peace without losing either their perspective or their sense of humour or both. Pearson has managed
to do that, and has helped a few others do the same. And it
is an accomplishment that official Washington is not likely to
forget for quite a while.'

Back in Ottawa, the Pearsons missed the many friends they
had made in Washington and the exciting life they had had
in one of the world's major capitals. Ottawa, by comparison,
was tranquil. The Pearsons were no longer obliged—or able
—to entertain to nearly the same extent as was expected of
the head of a diplomatic mission. Life became more normal
and, once they had adjusted to the changed atmosphere,
more comfortable. They purchased an old house, on Augusta
Street, in the Sandy Hill district of Ottawa, not far from the
East Block Parliament Hill offices of the External Affairs
Department. One little-publicized activity was Pearson's role,
with Maryon, in founding a dance club, the purpose of which
was to provide young (and often lonely) diplomats with an
opportunity to meet young Ottawans. Heads of missions were
not allowed to join, so that the maximum degree of informality
could be attained.

Although the nature of Pearson's work had changed, the
responsibilities were even greater. Pearson was now responsible for the management of the entire department, which had
grown greatly during the war years. In 1939 Canada had had
seven foreign missions; in 1945 it had twenty-two. The administrative problems associated with this rapid growth were
numerous, especially since organization had never been the
strong suit of the department. (In 1939, while posted in
London, Pearson visited Ottawa and reported on the situation to Vincent Massey: 'I have found out, if it needed

finding out, why so many things are not done that should be done. The Department, in one crude phrase, is in a mess . . . instead of the best, there must be almost the worst departmental organization.') Some of these problems were eased in 1946 when Mackenzie King realized that the burden of serving as his own foreign minister had become too great and he appointed Louis St Laurent, then the Minister of Justice, as Secretary of State for External Affairs. But the problems of administration were not solved, for this was not an area in which Pearson had much interest or ability. Arnold Heeney, who subsequently served under Pearson, wrote in his memoirs: 'Pearson had little time, indeed little taste, for administrative problems. His flair was for developing and negotiating avenues of solution, for action at the policy level. It has often been said and written of him that he disliked the business of running a department and that, in consequence, he was no good at it, and that he left to his officials . . . the unpleasant decisions of personnel management and housekeeping. There was much truth in this.' Although the department functioned reasonably well in terms of policy-making, many of the concerns of senior officials in Ottawa and at foreign posts—personnel, accommodation, allowances—remained unresolved.

Much of Pearson's attention during this period was focused on questions of post-war rehabilitation at home and abroad. He participated in interdepartmental meetings that examined the best way to reintegrate returning Canadian servicemen into the labour force without causing massive unemployment. The department was also actively involved in offering assistance to other countries that had been devastated by the war. In all this policy work, on which he thrived, Pearson was aided immeasurably by his close relationship with the new Secretary of State for External Affairs, Louis St Laurent. The minister had complete and profound confidence in Pearson, and the two tended to agree on most major matters. St Laurent invariably supported in Cabinet initiatives taken by Pearson, leaving Pearson free to concentrate on departmental measures without having to concern himself with getting his minister's approval. It was a harmonious and warm relationship that was to continue for many years— including the period 1948-57, when St Laurent was Prime Minister and Pearson the Secretary of State for External Affairs.

During these post-war years Pearson continued to be involved in the work of the new United Nations Organization. He had already displayed his diplomatic talents as chairman of a drafting sub-committee responsible for the development of procedures for an Interim Committee of the UN. Historian Robert Spender has described his efforts to reconcile the different views of the member-states: 'In sixteen meetings Mr Pearson steered it through a maze of legal complications with tact, discretion and flexibility of mind towards a reasonable compromise between giving the Committee so little power that [it] might as well never meet, and so much that its creation would radically alter the character of the UN and drive the U.S.S.R. out.' He also served as chairman of a special committee of the General Assembly established to study the question of creating a Jewish homeland in Palestine. A majority of states was determined to create the new state of Israel by a partition of Palestine, a move that was resisted by Arabs in the region. Pearson pushed for the formation of a four-nation working group, which he led, that ensured that the partition was done in as careful a manner as possible. For his efforts he was awarded the medallion of valour by the newly created state of Israel. The surrounding Arab states remained unalterably opposed to the partition, however; not even the most carefully drafted terms of partition could reconcile them to the loss of territory.

Although Pearson was becoming internationally recognized as a master diplomat, he was not always so regarded by Prime Minister King, who began to have second thoughts about Pearson's active role at the United Nations. King was very skeptical about the UN, just as he had been of the League of Nations, fearing that it would involve Canada in international commitments that would divert its energy and resources from more important problems at home. Pearson, on the other hand, believed that Canada had a responsibility to participate as actively as possible in any international activity that might lessen the chance of war's breaking out again. He felt that Canada's main national interest was to ensure that peace was maintained, and believed that the country should willingly accept international obligations to this end.

These conflicting views reached a head in 1948 over the issue of Korea. Canada was a member of the United Nations commission set up to supervise the holding of elections in Korea, which had been annexed by the Japanese in 1910. King was convinced that Canada should have nothing to do with this part of the world since, with the U.S., the U.S.S.R., and China all interested in the area, there was a danger that a dispute there could lead to world war. The Prime Minister even threatened to resign if Cabinet did not agree to end Canadian involvement in the commission. Pearson, in a highly unorthodox move, appealed to President Truman through the Canadian ambassador in Washington to persuade King to allow Canada to fulfil its UN responsibilities. This appeal from the American President, plus a counter-threat by St Laurent to resign if Canada were forced to withdraw, obliged the Prime Minister to back down. He continued to fill his diary, however, with comments that Pearson was taking too active a role in international activities and would soon get Canada involved in even more commitments. On one occasion the Prime Minister wrote: 'The truth is our country has no business trying to play a world role in the affairs of nations, the very location of some of which our people know little or nothing about. So far as External Affairs is concerned, they have been allowed to run far too much on Pearson's sole say-so, and Pearson himself [has been] moved far too much by the kind of influences that are brought to bear upon him. He is young, idealistic, etc., but has not responsibility. I am thankful I held responsibility for External Affairs as long as I did. At least I did not get the country into trouble by keeping it out of things it had no business to interfere with.'

By 1948 international tensions had increased to a point that had not been reached since just prior to the outbreak of the Second World War. The Soviet Union was using its veto power to frustrate the work of the UN Security Council, which was becoming increasingly ineffectual as a means of preventing war. The U.S.S.R. had lent active support to communist insurgents in Greece and Turkey who had attempted to topple the established governments and showed no signs of relinquishing its control over the Eastern European countries that it had occupied at the end of the war. The Russian invasion of Czechoslovakia in 1948 seemed to the countries of the West to be another example of Soviet aggression that might soon be directed towards Western

Europe. Several officials in Canada, Britain, and the United States, therefore, began to think of the possibility of forming a regional security alliance. Since the UN was powerless to take action to prevent aggression because of the existence of the veto power, a military defensive alliance of like-minded countries might be the next best thing. The British government was the first to propose the formation of such an alliance. With each member pledged to come to the aid of any other member that was attacked, the Soviet Union might be deterred from undertaking any aggressive actions against the countries of Western Europe.

The Canadian Department of External Affairs was highly enthusiastic about the idea. St Laurent and Pearson had become increasingly disillusioned with the United Nations, which had been reduced to ineffectiveness because of the lack of co-operation among the great powers. Speaking to a Toronto audience, Pearson said that there was less a feeling of 'one world' at that moment than at any time since A.D. 400. A regional security alliance would go a long way towards deterring aggression. By careful and cautious persuasion, St Laurent and Pearson convinced a reluctant Mackenzie King to authorize Canadian participation in the negotiations that eventually led to the formation of the North Atlantic Treaty Organization (NATO) in 1949. In April 1948 St Laurent gave a speech, largely written by Pearson, that showed Canada's determination to avoid isolationism and to opt for international commitments for the sake of preserving peace. 'I am sure,' he said, 'that it is the desire of the people of Canada that Canada should play its full part in creating and maintaining this overwhelming preponderance of moral, economic, and military force and the necessary unity for its effective use ... In the circumstances of the present, the organization of collective defense in this way is the most effective guarantee of peace.'

The decision by Canada to participate in NATO greatly increased the likelihood that the American Congress would approve U.S. participation as well. Now that Canada was involved, the United States could join without feeling that this was merely another in the long line of European requests for American assistance. James Reston of the *New York Times* wrote that the entry of Canada broadened the scope of the alliance into a wider association between two continents—'an offer of "association" not only with European nations, but with a popular and respected neighbor.' American participation was vital since the United States was the only Western country that possessed nuclear weapons, which were essential for effective deterrence. As the U.S. began to participate actively in the preliminary negotiations, Pearson used his close association with Dean Acheson, the American Secretary of State, to ensure that the NATO agreement contained the best possible provisions. One of the ideas Pearson advocated was that the organization should become involved in matters of economic and social as well as military co-operation. If it did not, he argued, the alliance would collapse once the specific military danger that led to its creation had passed. He was successful in getting his view incorporated into the final agreement as Article 2 (often referred to as the 'Canadian article'), but to his disappointment the alliance never did develop much beyond a purely military one. Nevertheless, Pearson later felt that the formation of NATO was one of the most important activities in which he had been involved, since it came at a time when international tensions were especially high. 'It was not the most exciting thing with which I was associated,' he told a friend, 'nor the most dramatic. It was not even the most immediately important thing. But in the long run I think it was the most important.'

Despite Prime Minister King's fears, recorded frequently in his diary, that Pearson was pursuing too active an international role for Canada, his respect for Pearson's ability led the Prime Minister to speak to Pearson 'of keeping in mind a possible future . . . in Canadian public life'. One of the arguments King used in attempting to persuade Pearson to return to Ottawa in 1946 was that 'it might be well to keep closely in touch with Canada with a view to getting into public life here.' King thought Pearson would make an excellent External Affairs minister and even toyed with the idea of Pearson's eventually becoming Prime Minister. (He expected that St Laurent would first succeed him as Prime Minister and would then soon retire from public life, leaving the way open for Pearson.) In his diary King wrote that he would 'rather have Pearson succeed me than anyone, when the time came.'

King was confident that Pearson, despite his protestations to the contrary, was anxious to enter political life, particularly if he could be Secretary of State for External Affairs. After a meeting in Paris in August 1946, he wrote in his diary: 'I spoke to Pearson about the possibilities the post might offer of his entering politics, which I think he would like to do.' St Laurent told King at one point that he believed Pearson was anxious to get into politics so that he could speak his own mind fully and argue questions himself rather than leaving this to his minister to do. The main problem, however, was that Pearson could not even consider the possibility of becoming foreign minister as long as King remained Prime

Minister, for their views on Canada's proper international role were too different. Pearson knew he would find it exceedingly difficult to work as minister with a Prime Minister who supported very reluctantly, if at all, Canadian participation in international organizations for collective security that Pearson regarded as indispensable. On one occasion, when Pearson's presence was requested at the United Nations to help resolve a dispute between India and Pakistan, King observed testily that, 'If necessary, our officials would have to choose between positions they held in Ottawa and positions they would like to have in the United Nations.' Referring to a memo submitted by Pearson, King complained that it was 'right along the lines that External Affairs has been taking for some time past, to get into every international situation and as much in the front of it as possible, not realizing what the appalling possibilities are.'

Mackenzie King retired in August 1948 and was succeeded as Prime Minister by Louis St Laurent. When St Laurent asked Pearson to become his Secretary of State for External Affairs, Pearson knew that he would be able to work comfortably with him. Political life, with its campaigning and controversies, did not appeal to Pearson. But the switch in jobs would not be all that abrupt; he would still be working with his old department, the only difference being that he would now be the political rather than the non-political head. He could view the change as the final step up the External Affairs ladder. Above all, he realized that as minister he would have far greater authority to determine the foreign policies for Canada that he considered important than he would have if he remained deputy minister. 'A civil servant,' he told a friend, 'can only go so far in determining policy. When the essential decisions are made, you're not even in the room. I want to be able to argue my points in Cabinet.' He felt that the world was at a crucial point, since the negotiations for the establishment of NATO were not yet concluded. 'I was now committed,' he wrote in his memoirs, 'to Atlantic collective security and the development of an Atlantic Community and I confess that the possibility of playing a political role under Mr St Laurent in this and related matters made a strong appeal to me.' Having weighed all these considerations, Pearson accepted the offer to enter political life.

On September 10, 1948, Lester Pearson was sworn in as Secretary of State for External Affairs. It was the culmination of a distinguished career in the Department of External Affairs, which he had entered twenty-one years earlier. As foreign minister, Pearson now had the responsibility for formulating Canada's foreign policy in the tense Cold War atmosphere that still enveloped the world, and the ensuing years brought with them several international crises in which Canada found itself playing a major part. That, however, was for the future. After his swearing-in, Pearson telephoned his mother in Toronto to tell her that he was now the Minister for External Affairs. Mrs Pearson, who had hoped when he first went to university that Lester would go on to become a minister of the gospel, said: 'Well, I am glad you have at last become a minister, if only a second-class one.' There could not be any swelled heads in the Pearson family.

Although Pearson was now a member of the Cabinet, it was also necessary for him to gain a seat in Parliament. He had established from the outset that he was not a die-hard Liberal. When asked by reporters, following his swearing-in, how long he had been a member of the Liberal party, he quipped: 'Since I was sworn in as a Minister a couple of hours ago.' If he sought election to Parliament as a Liberal, therefore, it was because he saw in the Liberal party an opportunity to accomplish something in the field that most interested him, foreign affairs. He had been a diplomat for too long not to be able to see both sides of an issue, and he could not bring himself to believe, as most successful politicians must, that there was only one party of truth and wisdom. For him people were clearly more important than party labels; he knew he could work effectively with St Laurent, and for that reason he agreed to become a member of the Liberal government.

The seat the party chose for him to contest was Algoma East, a rural riding in northern Ontario east of Sault Ste Marie and bordering on Georgian Bay. (Pearson was so unfamiliar with the area that he had to be shown on a map where the riding was located.) It had elected a Liberal to Parliament in every election since 1935. The sitting member was accordingly appointed to the Senate and a by-election was called. Pearson was clearly being treated as a very special candidate. Not only was a seat opened up for him but he was assured by the Prime Minister that, if he lost the by-election, he would be re-appointed to his post of Under-Secretary of State for External Affairs. In addition, a long-time friend, Walter Gordon, undertook to raise a sizeable annuity, to be made out in Maryon Pearson's name, so that he would not let financial worries prevent him from seeking office. This privileged treatment greatly reduced the insecurity Pearson felt in leaving the civil service for the uncertain world of politics.

Algoma East was not an easy riding in which to campaign. It consisted of some 20,000 square miles and had no single large community, which meant that candidates had to spend considerable time travelling throughout the constituency by car and train if they wished to meet many of the voters. The

Conservative party decided not to nominate a candidate to oppose Pearson, but both the CCF and Social Credit parties did their best to defeat him. Pearson's campaign was never really in doubt, however, and it received a boost when Prime Minister St Laurent himself visited the riding on his behalf. When the ballots were counted, Pearson was declared the winner by a margin of 3,276 votes.

Pearson did not have long to celebrate. Since he had to lead the Canadian delegation at a United Nations meeting in Paris the next day, his campaign manager drove him to Sudbury to catch the midnight train back to Ottawa and from there he flew to France. Pearson's hectic life as Secretary of State for External Affairs had begun.

3

Secretary of State for External Affairs

It soon became apparent that Lester Pearson was by no means a traditional politician. In his first public speech after making the jump from the civil service to politics, he demonstrated a trait that was to reappear in future years: an aversion to partisan politics. Foreign policy, he said, should be kept on a non-partisan basis to the greatest possible extent. 'After all, we are all Canadians, or should be, before we are Liberals, Conservatives, or CCFers, and before we are Quebeckers or Manitobans. So we should aim to face the outside world with a united front. Politics . . . should end at the water's edge.'

He was soon to find, however, that his distaste for partisan politics subjected him to a variety of pressures and created several problems. After all, the House of Commons was a political forum whether he liked it or not, and Pearson began to find himself under pressure to become part of it. His first speech in the House (on February 4, 1949) foreshadowed some of the dangers that lay ahead. Having been elevated rapidly to the most prestigious portfolio in the Cabinet, Pearson was worried that some of his fellow Liberal MPs might somewhat resent the fact that an 'outsider' had been given this 'plum' that would normally go to an experienced politician. As a result, the thought crossed his mind that it might help remove this feeling and convince them that he was a good 'party man' if he included in his maiden speech one remark of a partisan nature that would be likely to offend the Opposition. And so he asked why the Progressive Conservative party had not openly supported the creation of NATO during the previous debate. 'Is this Parliament not united in the objectives that we are seeking through this pact?' he asked. 'Or are any of us playing politics with peace at this time?'

The Conservative MPs reacted with indignation. Not only had the new minister violated the Parliamentary tradition that a member's maiden speech be non-partisan, but he had also accused them unjustly. The party had expressed no official opposition to NATO, and it was not long before they publicly supported it wholeheartedly. One Conservative yelled across the floor: 'The first speech and he plays politics!' Another made a more striking point: 'In view of the fact that foreign policy has been a matter of co-operation of all parties, does the minister think he is doing any good now by making this a political issue?' A third said: 'We expected more of him than this.' It was an inauspicious debut, and one that Pearson later regretted. But it was an indication of the hazards that the House of Commons held for someone with little political experience.

Despite this shaky start, Pearson soon warmed to his task and was highly successful when he concentrated on the field that he knew: foreign affairs. It was here that he felt he had a mission to perform. He had already been instrumental in convincing Mackenzie King of the need for Canada to play an active role in the formation of NATO, and he had participated in the first stages of the negotiations with the United States and Great Britain while still Under-Secretary. The final details of the treaty were negotiated primarily at the

ambassadorial level in Washington, where Hume Wrong presented Canada's case that the treaty should provide for
co-operation in political, social, and economic questions, as
well as in the military field. However, the U.S. Secretary of
State, Dean Acheson, was concerned with winning the support of a hesitant Congress for the military co-operation that
was to be the basis of the treaty; he viewed Pearson's concern
with non-military co-operation as little more than 'typical
Canadian moralizing'. The Canadian negotiators succeeded
in gaining acceptance for an article providing for economic
collaboration among the member-states, but in practice little
came of this provision, since the Americans in particular
regarded NATO as simply a military alliance. But in 1949 it
was understandable that military matters were of top priority,
and the creation of a defensive alliance was viewed as a
considerable accomplishment when the foreign ministers of
the twelve participating countries met in Washington on
April 4, 1949, to sign the North Atlantic Treaty.* Pearson,
representing the Canadian government, believed that the
NATO alliance was essential for world security, especially
since the Soviet Union's invasion of Czechoslovakia in 1948,
which had convinced many Western countries that only a
firm military alliance, based on U.S. nuclear power, would
deter further Soviet aggression. The key article of the treaty
provided that each member-nation would consider an armed
attack on any other member as an armed attack against all.

The dignified atmosphere of the signing ceremony was
heightened by a band of U.S. Marines playing soft music in

---

* The original members of NATO were Belgium, Canada, Denmark, France, Iceland,
Italy, Luxembourg, the Netherlands, Norway, Portugal, the United Kingdom, and
the United States. Greece and Turkey subsequently joined the Alliance in 1952, and
the Federal Republic of Germany became its fifteenth member in 1955.

the background. (Several participants noted the irony in the fact that, among its selections, the band played 'It ain't Necessarily so' and 'I Got Plenty of Nothin'' from *Porgy and Bess.*) As each of the foreign ministers present was to make a brief statement before the signing, Dean Acheson asked each which language he would use so that the appropriate interpreters would be present. Pearson relieved the tension felt by all by replying that he would speak 'North American English with a French accent'. His comments reflected his conviction of the importance of the agreement. 'Last week,' he said, 'the Parliament of Canada, with only two dissenting voices, endorsed the treaty which we sign here today. This virtual unanimity reflected the views of the Canadian people who feel deeply and instinctively that this treaty is not a pact for war, but a pledge for peace and progress.'

The Canadian government had, in fact, been amazingly successful in obtaining the support of the Canadian people for a policy that dramatically reversed the pre-1939 policy of isolationism. In large part this was owing to a very real fear of war and a realization that only by banding together could the countries of North America and Western Europe do what they had failed to do in 1939: prevent aggression. Pearson argued the case for collective security passionately and eloquently, but the battle was already won. The Ottawa *Evening Journal* noted that during one debate his lucid account of the Treaty and its background fell short of its full effect because the House was already in agreement. Pearson was caught 'with a persuasive text in his hands but nobody to persuade.'

The ten years during which Lester Pearson was Secretary of State for External Affairs was for Canadian foreign policy a 'golden decade'. In large part this was because of favourable world circumstances: Britain, France, Germany, and

Japan had all been devastated by war while Canada, its economy strengthened by the war effort, had emerged as the third or fourth strongest power in the world. Without this position of relative strength, Canada could have accomplished little even with the best of intentions. But accomplishments also depend on a willingness to make the most of existing resources and opportunities, and this Pearson was able to provide. In his personal scale of priorities the need to avoid war was always paramount. 'You may say that peace isn't a policy, it's a prayer,' he told an interviewer in 1949. 'Maybe. But that prayer should be the ultimate objective of everything we do in our relations with other countries—to avoid conflict and maintain peace.' When Canada's capabilities were combined with Pearson's determination to put them to the best use, the result was a foreign policy that saw Canada playing for the first time in its peace-time history an active role on the international stage.

Another important factor in Canada's new role in world affairs was the strong relationships Pearson developed with the Prime Minister, Parliament, and the public. Whereas Mackenzie King had wanted to keep control of foreign policy in his own hands, Louis St Laurent, who respected Pearson, was willing to give him virtually a free rein in most important matters. Pearson could therefore devote almost all his attention to the international scene without worrying about how to convince the Prime Minister that he was doing the right thing. Indeed, their attitudes towards the international role that Canada should play were so similar that it was often difficult to tell where the influence of one ended and that of the other began. The new Secretary of State also attempted to promote discussion of foreign policy in the House of Commons and its committees, something that previous governments had shied away from. Arnold Heeney wrote in his memoirs that these years were 'in many ways the golden age of Canadian diplomacy and Pearson enjoyed enormous prestige amongst all members of Parliament.' Finally, Pearson placed great stress on public education. As one of the most sought-after speakers in the Cabinet, he was constantly explaining to audiences across the country what he was trying to accomplish. In speech after speech he emphasized the important contribution that Canada could make to world peace and security, and the need to set aside purely national interests for those of the larger world community. It was not long before internationalism was as fashionable and widespread a view in Canada as isolationism had been only fifteen years earlier. Some, though by no means all, of the credit for this shift in attitude was due to Pearson and the St Laurent government.

The first international crisis to face Pearson in his new role as foreign minister involved the threatened break-up of the Commonwealth. The source of the problem was India. Having just obtained independence from Britain, India wished to establish a republican system of government to symbolize that independence. The question was: could a country whose constitution made no provision for the Crown remain in the Commonwealth, whose members had all been linked in the past by their common allegiance to the British monarch? Australia and New Zealand thought not. As the foreign ministers from the Commonwealth countries rushed to an emergency meeting in London in April 1949, it appeared that membership in the organization might be denied to one of the largest states in Asia. Lester Pearson and the Canadian delegation led the fight to arrive at a compromise, which was finally reached after six difficult days of secret negotiations.

India agreed to recognize the British monarch as the Head of the Commonwealth (although not as the King of India) and India's continuing membership in the Commonwealth was recognized by the other members. The agreement, Pearson later stated, showed that the Commonwealth was sufficiently strong to meet changing conditions: 'The nations who compose it remain joined not by written compact or by some imposed link but by other and stronger bonds.' The crucial role played by Pearson was tacitly recognized later in the year when India's Prime Minister Nehru, during a visit to Canada, referred to 'the spirt of understanding' shown by the Canadian government at the April meeting. Canada, Nehru said, had emerged as a pioneer in the evolution of a Commonwealth association based on complete freedom, unfettered by an outside control.

It was only one year later, in January 1950, that Canada again played a part in establishing a new purpose and orientation for the Commonwealth. For the first time the Commonwealth foreign ministers met in an Asian country—newly independent Ceylon—and concentrated on matters of particular interest to Asia. The result of the meeting was the Colombo Plan (named after the Ceylonese capital where the meetings were held), under which the economically developed member-countries joined together in an attempt to raise the standard of living of the poorer Commonwealth countries in Asia. Pearson, although not one of the most enthusiastic participants at Colombo, eventually recommended that Canada contribute $25 million to India and Pakistan—a previously unheard-of sum of money for such a purpose, which marked the effective beginning of Canada's foreign-aid program. He explained to Canadians why their country should become involved in foreign aid. If Asia were not to be conquered by

Communism, he said, it was up to the countries of the free democratic world to prove that they could do more than the Soviet Union to improve the standard of living of the people of Asia. But while his support of foreign aid was at first motivated by political considerations of this kind, his Methodist-inspired humanism soon came to the fore. By 1955 he was defending foreign-aid programs on humanitarian grounds: 'If we of the West provide material aid only or primarily for cold-war motives, we are likely to fail in achieving any good and permanent results.' Little by little a new and increasingly important aspect of Canada's external relations was developing.

The second international crisis in which Canada became involved was not resolved as easily. In 1950 the Canadian government was in the process of negotiating with the newly formed People's Republic of China for the establishment of diplomatic relations when the outbreak of the Korean War forced such political considerations to the background. The invasion of South Korea by North Korea was regarded by Canada as an act of naked aggression. When the Security Council of the United Nations urged its members to supply military units to repel the invasion, Pearson was quick to respond. Here, he felt, was an opportunity for collective international action to stop aggression—the very purpose of the United Nations. Canada promptly agreed to make three destroyers available to the UN naval force, and to airlift supplies and arms to South Korea. But Cabinet was not as quick to agree to Pearson's proposal that Canada recruit a volunteer brigade to serve with the UN forces in Korea. After several months of hesitation, when it became clear that the Canadian public favoured such a move, the government finally accepted his advice. The Korean War offered Pearson an opportunity to stress a theme that he repeated frequently in the years that followed: the need for a permanent UN military force to deter aggression. Other countries, he said, should follow Canada's lead in earmarking a portion of their forces that might be made available to the UN for collective defence so that 'there would be ready throughout the free world national contingents for a UN force which could be quickly brought together in the face of future emergency.'

Not only was this hope never realized, but the UN force in Korea soon discredited itself in the eyes of many. Its American commander, General MacArthur, believed that the North Korean army could be completely destroyed if his forces crossed the 38th Parallel into North Korea and pursued the enemy as far as possible—to the Chinese border if necessary. Pearson was appalled. He feared that any military action near the Yalu River, which separated Korea from Manchuria, would provoke China's entry into the war. And he suspected MacArthur of secretly hoping for a confrontation with the Chinese that would result in the overthrow of the Communist régime in Peking. In private conversations with Dean Acheson and other U.S. officials, Pearson and his colleagues stressed that the conflict had to be kept 'localized' (in Korea). If China were provoked into entering the war, the credibility of the UN force as a purely defensive body would be ruined, and with it the prestige of the United Nations as a collective security organization. General MacArthur paid no heed. On November 24 he began his 'end-the-war campaign' with a major drive towards the Yalu River. As Pearson had feared, Chinese forces quickly counter-attacked, driving back the UN troops and nearly overwhelming them. The war had entered a new and ominous phase.

As the fighting continued, Canada was disturbed by a

remark of President Truman's that seemed to suggest that the U.S. was prepared to use nuclear weapons to end the war. This so worried Pearson that he not only asked for clarification of the remark through diplomatic channels but also spoke out publicly. The use of nuclear weapons, he said, might possibly destroy the cohesion and unity of purpose of the Atlantic Community. 'Certainly its use for the second time against an Asian people would dangerously weaken the links that remain between the Western world and the peoples of the East.'

In his department's annual report of 1950, Pearson showed his frustration over the failure of the United Nations to achieve its goals, while repeating the dogged optimism he exhibited throughout his career: 'The year ends in crisis and disappointed hopes. But that should be no reason for despair or for slackening of effort. Rather it should call forth from all Canadians the energies and sacrifices which will be needed if we are to be successful in building a world where peace will be secure.'

Canada's efforts were henceforth directed towards bringing an end to the hostilities. Pearson agreed to participate on a three-man cease-fire committee set up by the President of the UN General Assembly in December 1950. The Committee drew up a statement of principles for a cease-fire and began indirect discussions with Peking. But just when it seemed that an agreement was possible, the U.S. introduced at the United Nations a resolution to condemn Communist China as an 'aggressor'. Pearson called it 'premature and unwise' but eventually decided to support the resolution in order to maintain the solidarity of the Western alliance. Despite his best efforts (which included toning down some of the more provocative phrases in the resolution), peace seemed further

The president of the General Assembly of the United Nations reading a memorial tribute on U.N. Day, October 24, 1952.

away than ever. Even the traditional non-partisan approach to foreign policy within Canada was beginning to be shattered: the CCF moved a motion of non-confidence in the government for supporting a resolution that would place a further obstacle in the way of a negotiated settlement.

Pearson's diplomatic talents and his popularity among UN delegates were recognized in 1952 when he was elected president of the General Assembly. In addition to the formal, time-consuming task of presiding over debates, Pearson's main preoccupation was to find some way of resolving the conflict in Korea. The first problem involved proposals for the repatriation of prisoners, on which agreement was necessary before a cease-fire could be instituted. The U.S. Secretary of State, Dean Acheson, had submitted one set of proposals and Krishna Menon, the foreign minister of India, had submitted another. Pearson undertook the delicate task of mediating between these two strong personalities. Acheson did not appreciate his efforts and wrote in his memoirs how he had had to guard 'against proposals of two adroit operators, Krishna Menon ... and Lester B. Pearson'. He suggested that Pearson had been negative and obstructionist and had joined Menon's 'cabal'. In his own memoirs Pearson disputed Acheson's allegations of duplicity. Nevertheless he gave Menon encouragement, canvassed other delegations to gain their views, and assisted in the drafting and redrafting of the Indian resolution, which was eventually accepted by the General Assembly. During this complex negotiating the importance of Pearson's experience and contacts was very evident. As one observer wrote later: 'The trick, it seems, is to walk through the delegates' lounges at the UN whispering the right thing to the right person at precisely the right moment.'

In 1953 both sides, locked in a military stalemate in Korea, finally agreed to sign an armistice. The next year the foreign ministers of the countries involved met at Geneva to attempt to arrive at a political settlement. Pearson urged both sides to accept the UN resolution calling for a union of all Korean people under a government chosen by them, but both the Soviet Union and North Korea added conditions that were unacceptable to the South Koreans. The military stalemate remained and overt hostilities were not resumed, but the UN had been unable to achieve a lasting political solution.

Nevertheless Pearson did not lose his faith in the United Nations as a symbol of the world-wide community that was his main goal. In large part he was aided by his basic pragmatism, which led him to believe that even second-best solutions to problems were better than none at all. The UN might not have brought about a political solution to the Korean war, but it had at least halted the invasion by North Korea and had brought an end to the fighting. 'There are times, Mr Chairman,' he said during one particularly trying day at the UN, 'when we must all feel as though, in the international field, we were pushing through a bitter and blinding blizzard. But it would be fatal to yield to the temptation to merely sit it out.' His confidence was also sustained by his belief in the importance of the economic and social organizations within the UN, in whose establishment he had been so actively involved. It might not always be possible to solve political problems, but he wanted the UN to move towards 'economic and social progress and away from poverty ... toward the progressive realization of human rights and the dignity and worth of the individual person.' Unlike some idealists, Pearson did not hesitate to match his words with action. Canada soon gained the reputation in foreign circles as one of the most internationalist of countries, ready to support almost all UN initiatives. Canadian diplomats became, if not the power-brokers at the UN, some of the chief mediators and innovators whenever problems arose.

Perhaps the best indication of Pearson's prestige at the UN was that in 1953 he came within an inch of becoming the organization's second Secretary-General. The first, Trygve Lie, had served since 1946, and Pearson's name figured prominently among those being considered as his successor. Although the Soviet Union had been opposed when he was suggested for the position in 1946, the *New York Times* carried a front-page story that the Soviets were now prepared to accept him. (Ironically, the Americans were not enamoured with Pearson at this time because of the independent approach he had followed over Korea; but they realized he would be an excellent choice.) Pearson discussed the situation with Prime Minister St Laurent and both agreed that he should accept if the Security Council nominated him, even though St Laurent was particularly loathe to lose one of his top ministers on the eve of a general election. As for Pearson, he felt it would be his duty to serve if called upon, since he still viewed the UN as the world's greatest hope for lasting peace. On March 19 the Security Council voted: Pearson received nine votes compared to five for his nearest rival. But the Soviet Union used its veto power against him on the grounds that he was too closely allied with the United States. Pearson was disappointed. Although not concerned with considerations of prestige, he viewed the position of Secretary-General as an important one through which a great deal could be accomplished.

1953 was a particularly tiring year for Pearson. In addition to looking after his regular responsibilities as foreign minister, he was required to spend a great deal of time in New York to attend to his important duties as President of the General Assembly. On top of the preoccupations of his possibly becoming the next Secretary-General, there were political concerns at home to engage his mind. 1953 was an election year in Canada, which meant that Pearson had to take to the campaign trail. The St Laurent government was still highly popular and was returned with a comfortable majority. Pearson had no difficulty in winning re-election in Algoma East.

A major Canadian contribution to the United Nations during this period, one that is often overlooked, was the role played by Canada in making the UN a more truly 'universal' organization. When the UN was established in 1946, it had fifty-one members. In the years that followed, countries such as Ireland, Italy, Austria, and Finland applied for membership but were refused. The Soviets blocked the admission of additional countries since the U.S. objected to membership for Outer Mongolia, believing it to be little more than a Russian colony.

Pearson, about to leave on an official visit to the Soviet Union, asked the head of the Canadian delegation to the UN, Paul Martin, to call on the Soviet representative to discuss travel plans and also to find out if this deadlock could not be resolved. To Martin's astonishment the Soviet response was positive. After a period of negotiation a 'package deal' was arranged that admitted sixteen new nations to the international body. It was the first major increase in membership since the creation of the United Nations, and one that prepared the way for future growth. Martin justly received much of the credit for the behind-the-scenes work that led to the deal, but he admitted freely that, in the beginning, 'It was Mike's idea.'

Although Pearson never abandoned hope for the United Nations, it was clear to him that NATO occupied a particularly important place in Canada's foreign-policy priorities. If collective security could not be achieved through the UN where the great powers could use their veto right to block action, the nations of the Western world had to seek their security in regional alliances of like-minded countries. That was the main reason for Pearson's avid interest in NATO, which was also important because it was composed of three of the countries on whom Canada relied the most and with which it had the closest ties—Britain, France, and above all the United States. Since the leader of the Western coalition was the United States, it was essential for Canada to be able to influence Washington along desirable lines. The 'first principle of Canadian diplomacy' for Pearson was therefore to encourage the U.S. to support actively the Western coalition against the Soviet Union and not retreat into the isolationism that had dominated American foreign policy before the Second World War. Pearson became chairman of the North Atlantic Council in 1951, at a time when the organization was building up its military strength to counter any attack from the Soviet Union. In 1954 he led the Canadian delegation to London, where it was agreed to admit West Germany to the Western alliance.

In 1955 the NATO leaders made a significant decision: they wanted NATO to become more than just a military alliance. Pearson, who had advocated all along the formation of a true 'North Atlantic Community' in which members would co-operate in political, economic, and cultural as well as military matters, was chosen as one of three men* to study

* The others were Halvard Lange and Dr Gaetano Martino, the foreign ministers of Norway and Italy.

how these non-military aims might best be met. In speeches throughout the Western world the Canadian foreign minister told audiences that NATO was at the crossroads of its existence. 'If it is to go forward, and in the right direction,' he said, 'it must concentrate on ways and means of bringing its members closer together politically, without weakening its defence unity and strength.' He and his two NATO colleagues—soon referred to as the 'three wise men of NATO' —urged that the NATO council be given more power and that consultations be increased so that no member would think of taking action that affected the others without prior discussion. But all these hopes of turning NATO into a true North Atlantic Community, united by common ideals and interests, collapsed. The goal was highly idealistic and not well defined to begin with. In addition, the Americans viewed NATO as a military organization first and foremost and were reluctant to consider extending allied co-operation into other fields. When six European countries (France, Germany, Italy, Holland, Belgium, and Luxembourg) decided to form the European Economic Community in 1957, a process of integration began that was to leave Canada on the outside. Pearson had long felt that if NATO were merely a military alliance, it would slowly collapse when its members felt less threatened by the Soviet Union. That is precisely what happened in the late 1960s. The refusal of other countries to co-operate in the creation of a true North Atlantic Community—and his failure to convince even some of his own Canadian colleagues of the merits of such a plan—was one of the major failures of Pearson's diplomatic efforts and a great personal disappointment.

When, after the Second World War, the United States emerged as the most powerful country in the world and

Great Britain was preoccupied with the task of rebuilding its economy, Canada quite naturally developed closer and closer ties with its southern neighbour. Before the war Britain had been Canada's best customer; by 1956 the United States market consumed some 60 per cent of all Canadian exports, more than three times the amount purchased from Canada by Britain. Slowly but surely Canadian society was becoming Americanized. The steady penetration of American magazines, books, radio, and now television gradually led most Canadians to identify themselves, at least subconsciously, with the United States. The U.S., leading the free world against Communism, was a country to be admired; its presidential elections, its movie stars, and its business know-how were objects of fascination. Canadians cherished their political independence but still felt more like brothers than neighbours to the Americans.

Pearson recognized that Canada had to accept the reality of being a North American nation, especially after his hopes for a North Atlantic Community were dashed. He realized too that it was upon the U.S. that the freedom of the Western world depended in the 1950s, and that Canada's supreme foreign-policy task was to influence the American government to adopt wise policies. But Pearson was slightly ahead of some of his countrymen in realizing what this new relationship with the United States would mean for Canada. In a 1951 speech he shocked many Canadians by suggesting that, despite the close ties, 'the days of relatively easy and automatic political relations with our neighbour are, I think, over.' He realized that the more contacts there were between the two countries, the more conflicts there would be. And since the actions of the U.S. were so important for the world, Canada would have to express its disagreement whenever it felt that the American government was steering a wrong course. To Pearson's amazement, newspaper accounts of his speech gave little attention either to the reasons for his comment or to his earlier observation that Canada's destiny was inseparable from that of the western hemisphere. Headlines across the country read very much like the one that said 'Pearson criticizes Americans—says easy relations with them are over.' Many Canadians had become so accustomed to thinking in terms of co-operation with the United States that they almost instinctively regarded anyone who differed with the U.S. as somewhat disloyal to their best neighbour. (On the other hand, Pearson also received considerable support from some Canadians for having 'stood up to the Americans'. This 'extravagant praise', as Pearson described it to a friend, worried him more than the criticism, for it demonstrated to him 'how easy it would be to work up a strong anti-American feeling in this country at this time'.)

In the months that followed, Pearson set out to explain to his countrymen what he had meant: while Canada should do nothing that would weaken the Western coalition, it had a moral duty to disagree whenever it felt the U.S. was mistaken. Canada had ample cause for disagreement in the years ahead. In 1954 the American Secretary of State, John Foster Dulles, developed for NATO a doctrine of 'massive retaliation' whereby the United States would counter any aggression against the West by a huge nuclear attack. Pearson stressed that no such action should be taken without consultation with the other NATO members or else the alliance would be meaningless. Above all, Canada did not want to become wholly dependent upon the U.S. and unable to infleunce American policy. His criticism of the American position led to the following favourable editorial in the *New*

York Times: 'What Mr Pearson's frank statement has done is to stress again the importance of Canada in our security and the necessity of keeping her fully informed and winning her support.'

A more serious crisis arose the same year when Communist China began shelling two off-shore islands in the Pacific that the Americans were determined to protect. Before long it appeared that the United States might use armed force against China if the attacks were extended to the island of Formosa. If the Soviet Union then came to the aid of China, the result would be world war. Although there was some pressure from Canadian public opinion and the press for Canada to commit itself immediately to aid the United States in the event of war, Pearson refused, believing it would be 'unutterable folly' to allow the islands to become the cause of a major conflict. He urged the U.S. to refer the matter to the United Nations instead. Although both the Conservative and Social Credit parties in Parliament supported the U.S. stand, Pearson stated unequivocally that Canada disagreed with the United States on this crucial matter (for only on crucial matters did he think Canada should openly express its disagreement) and would not be committed by any American action in the Pacific. The expected war never came, for the Chinese gradually ended their shelling and the crisis died a natural death. However, the 'off-shore islands dispute' showed that Pearson was determined to stand up to the United States when he felt it was necessary. (Ironically, he was to be accused of 'selling out to the Americans' less than ten years later when he determined that Canada's armed forces should use U.S. nuclear weapons.)

In 1955 Lester Pearson made history by becoming the first foreign minister from a NATO country to visit the Soviet

Union. Tensions between the U.S.S.R. and the West were particularly high at that time, for Moscow had recently agreed to supply Egypt with arms. It appeared to many Western observers that the Soviets were deliberately trying to upset the precarious balance of power in the Middle East between Israel and the Arab states. By agreeing to go to Russia, Pearson showed that Canada wanted to ease cold-war tensions. To do that, it was first necessary for the two sides to understand each other better.

Pearson first received the invitation while he was in San Francisco to mark the tenth anniversary of the signing of the United Nations charter. After one of the afternoon meetings, he ran into the Soviet foreign minister, who—to Pearson's great surprise—invited him to visit Russia. The Prime Minister agreed that the invitation should be accepted and on September 30, 1955, Pearson and his wife left Ottawa in a Canadian air force plane with a small group of government officials and journalists. After stops in London, Paris (where the Pearsons visited their son Geoffrey, who had joined the Department of External Affairs), and Berlin, they arrived in Moscow on October 5. Their hectic schedule began later in the day. After paying a courtesy call on the Soviet foreign minister and visiting the Canadian embassy, the Pearsons were guests of honour at the Bolshoi theatre for a performance of the ballet *Don Quixote*. The Pearsons were seated in the former royal box of the famous theatre. A spotlight was trained on them and the audience gave them a standing ovation. Pearson turned and whispered to one of his companions: 'It makes me feel like the Czar. The Little Elgin [movie] theatre in Ottawa was never like this.' In the days that followed, the Canadian delegation attended receptions, banquets, soccer matches, agricultural exhibitions, and lunch-

With Nikita Khrushchev in Russia, October 1955.

eons, when it was not meeting with Soviet officials to discuss political or economic matters. On October 7 the exacting schedule prepared for Pearson by the Russians allowed him exactly twelve minutes of free time during the day and evening. Reflecting on his trip later, and remembering the famous book about the Russian revolution called *Ten Days That Shook the World*, Pearson said: 'If I ever do write one about my visit to Russia, it will be called *The Eight Days That Shook the Pearsons*.'

While in Moscow, Pearson expressed the wish to attend a Protestant church service. His hosts willingly obliged and he was taken on a Sunday evening to a crowded Baptist church. To Pearson's surprise he was seated on the platform with the minister, who proceeded to introduce him to the congregation. 'What is he saying?' Pearson asked George Ignatieff, the Canadian official beside him, who could speak Russian. 'He is telling them you are going to preach to them,' Ignatieff answered. Pearson unwillingly complied, using as his text 'Blessed are the peacemakers'—the theme of peacemaking being a very popular one with his Russian hosts. The congregation, who listened attentively, broke spontaneously into a hymn when he finished. To Pearson's amusement the melody was that of 'Rescue the Perishing'.

After a sightseeing trip to Leningrad, Pearson flew to the Crimea to meet Premier Khrushchev at his vacation retreat. After a hair-raising fifty-mile drive at high speed along tortuous mountain roads, Pearson and the three diplomats accompanying him arrived at Yusopof Palace, overlooking the Black Sea, where Khrushchev was staying. 'Proleterian luxury de luxe,' Pearson said when he saw it. When he met Khrushchev shortly after eight o'clock that night, the Russian leader bluntly attacked NATO as a threat to the Soviet

Union. Pearson tried to convince him that NATO was a purely defensive organization, but Khrushchev retorted that when people attacked others, they always said it was for defensive purposes. Pearson firmly replied that, 'So far as Canada is concerned, we will not attack anyone nor will we take part with other people in an attack on anyone.' At ten o'clock the formal discussions ended and the group adjourned to the dining room for a banquet that proved to be gruelling for the Canadians. Khrushchev proposed toast after toast of strong Russian vodka, in which the visitors felt compelled to join in order not to appear impolite. Some time after midnight, nineteen toasts later, the Canadians were finally allowed to take their leave. The next day, as they returned to the airfield, they were too exhausted from their hectic schedule and lack of sleep, and too queasy from the hairpin turns of the drive, to appreciate the historic sights that were shown them on the way. When one of the Soviet escorts pointed to a monument erected to commemorate a Russian marshal who had lost an eye defeating the Turks, Pearson remarked: 'You might raise a monument to me back at that place where I lost my stomach.' In his light-hearted way, Pearson later commented that he had endured 'conviviality beyond the line of duty'. At the end of the visit, one Canadian journalist reported that 'Mr Pearson was—and looked—utterly exhausted. His seven-day visit to Russia had been tiring, and the previous day had been the worst one of all.'*

---

* Despite his extremely demanding schedule, Pearson continued to display the enthusiasm and sense of humour his friends found so engaging. But his long-time acquaintances did notice that his life as a public figure made a mark on him. After a meeting with Pearson in Ottawa in 1955, Arnold Heeney, Canada's Ambassador to Washington, wrote in his private journal: 'LBP is in fair form . . . He continues to be constantly vigorous and interested and stimulating and cheerful. But over the years, although consistently friendly and satisfactory with me, he is increasingly impersonal—a deep one whose secret self very few, if any, can know.'

Nevertheless the trip was a very useful one for Pearson, and for Canada. The Russians agreed to buy 400,000 tons of wheat a year for three years. The Soviet newspaper *Pravda* stated that the visit would 'undoubtedly contribute to strengthening Soviet-Canadian good-neighbourly relations', and indeed, comments made by the two countries about each other in the years that followed lacked much of the cold-war bitterness of the early 1950s. Above all, Pearson returned to Canada with a new awareness of the Soviet Union and its leaders. His main impression of the country was one of 'massive power on the part of the state, of great collective strength, and of inflexible purpose.' But he was impressed by the sincerity of Khrushchev's fears that the West planned to attack the U.S.S.R. and by his assurances that the Soviet Union harboured no aggressive intentions itself. Pearson began to appreciate the extent to which each side was ignorant of the other—and to realize that this ignorance led to mutual suspicions. He was struck by the fact that the Russians genuinely desired peaceful coexistence with the West, at least temporarily, and were not the blatant aggressors many people in the Western world believed them to be. He concluded that the West would have to remain militarily strong but that NATO should begin to place more emphasis on economic and political (not just military) co-operation, in order to disprove the Soviet belief that NATO was an aggressive military organization. The Cold War was not yet over, but Pearson was one of the first Western statesmen to see that a reduction in tensions was possible if the West acted wisely.

Elsewhere in the world storm clouds were gathering. In the Middle East an uneasy truce had been in existence since 1949 between the newly created state of Israel and its surrounding

Arab neighbours, who were dedicated to its destruction. The periodic armistice violations increased in intensity in 1955 as both sides conducted raids and reprisals. Then came the news that the Soviet Union had agreed to supply Egypt with arms. Since the United States and France were supplying arms to Israel (as Canada and other NATO countries had also done), it began to appear that a conflict between Egypt and Israel might expand into a world war between East and West.

The Middle East war that many had been fearing finally broke out in 1956. Its origins were confusing and complex. President Nasser wished to obtain U.S. and British financial support for the construction of the Aswan Dam in Egypt, and these negotiations were completed in July 1956. But only a few days later the U.S. Secretary of State, John Foster Dulles, decided to withdraw American support from the project. He was disturbed by the increasingly friendly relations between Egypt and the Soviet Union, and angered by Egypt's recent recognition of Communist China. His petulance only drove Egypt further into the Soviet camp. On July 26 President Nasser announced that the Egyptian government had nationalized the Suez Canal Company and would use the canal tolls to underwrite the construction of the dam. Both Britain and France had important financial interests in the Suez Canal; the nationalization particularly angered British Prime Minister Anthony Eden, who began to speak of the possibility of using force if Nasser did not reconsider. On October 29, with the issue still before the United Nations, Israeli forces moved into Egypt and towards the canal; the next day Britain and France stated that, if both sides did not cease fire and withdraw from the canal, they would themselves occupy key points in order to keep the traffic moving. Egypt rejected this ultimatum. On October 31 British and French bombers began attacking selected points in the canal zone. Thus began the greatest international crisis since the Korean War.

The Canadian government was worried—and displeased—for a number of reasons. In the first place, it had received no advance warning of Britain's intentions: St Laurent first learned of the British and French ultimatum to Egypt from a wire-service report. Later he received a secret cable from Eden explaining the reason for Britain's action and seeking Canada's support. St Laurent was furious and wished to send off an indignant reply; Pearson and his officials convinced him to soften the tone somewhat but to leave no doubt that Canada was displeased by the lack of prior consultation and was not prepared to support Britain automatically. St Laurent's reply expressed Pearson's views that the ultimate danger was that both the Soviet Union and the United States would become involved in the conflict. But the immediate threat was three-fold: the possibility of a serious division in the Commonwealth because of the strong opposition of some members, such as India, to Britain's action; the growing divergence of policy between the United States and Britain, whose co-operation was the basis of the Western alliance and whose disagreement would put Canada in the difficult position of having to choose between them; and the damage that had been done to the United Nations by military action undertaken at a time when the Security Council was in the process of examining the dispute. All of Canada's most important diplomatic relations were endangered. If it supported Britain and France, it would risk antagonizing the United States, as well as important Commonwealth countries in the third world, who regarded the invasion of Egypt as 'imperialist aggression'. On the other hand, if Canada opposed Britain and France it would be accused of disloyalty towards its two mother countries.

The tactic that Pearson chose was to avoid any condemnations and, instead, to seek to end the crisis as quickly as possible through the United Nations. The way in which he hoped to do this was through the creation of an international police force that would separate the combatants. In addition to bringing an end to the fighting, this would have the advantage of allowing Britain and France to withdraw their forces before they were formally condemned by the General Assembly. Pearson first raised the idea at a Cabinet meeting on November 1, and St Laurent urged him to fly to New York immediately to see what he could do. The idea of an international force was not a new one, but it had been dismissed in past years as impractical. The situation was now so serious that Pearson hoped a majority of UN members would agree to the creation of such a force.

Pearson arrived at the United Nations shortly before the dinner recess. (A heavy fog in New York almost prevented his plane from landing at all.) He immediately asked to have his name added to the list of speakers but found that there were twenty-one others ahead of him. They were debating an American resolution calling for a cease-fire and a withdrawal of all invading forces. Pearson quickly decided that the American proposal was inadequate, for it made no provision for supervising or enforcing the cease-fire. He concluded that Canada should abstain on the vote, for he could not hope to win acceptance for his own proposal if Canada were on record as favouring an American position with which Britain and France were certain to be opposed. Meanwhile, Pearson's colleagues canvassed other delegates in the corridors and the lounge to learn their views; by midnight they compared their notes and concluded that a resolution for a UN peace-keeping force would be well supported. It was early in the morning by the time the U.S. resolution was voted upon. Pearson, after checking with St Laurent by telephone, abstained but asked for the floor in order to explain his abstention, as was allowed by the rules of procedure. One of his Canadian colleagues, Geoffrey Murray, later described his preparation for that speech: 'He scribbled notes for that all-important statement . . . while he sat at the Canada desk, frequently interrupted by urgent consultations and messages, always in the din of debate since the draw had placed us right under the speakers' lectern. Few public servants I have known, even seasoned United Nations pros, had the power of concentration to work so effectively in that kind of turmoil.'

When his turn to speak finally came, Pearson told the delegates that he wondered what use there was in passing a resolution to bring about a cease-fire if there was not also some arrangement to police the cease-fire and to prepare for a political settlement. He continued:

I would therefore have liked to see a provision in this resolution . . . authorizing the Secretary-General to begin to make arrangements with member governments for a United Nations force large enough to keep these borders at peace while a political settlement is being worked out. I regret exceedingly that time has not been given to follow up this idea, which was mentioned also by the representative of the United Kingdom in his first speech, and I hope that even now, when action on the resolution has been completed, it may not be too late to give consideration to this matter. My own government would be glad to recommend Canadian participation in such a United Nations force, a truly international peace and police force.

It was 4:20 a.m. when the Assembly finally adjourned for the night. Before going to bed Pearson talked briefly with the

UN Secretary-General, Dag Hammarskjold, whose support would be absolutely essential if a peace-keeping force were to be created. They met again at lunch that day. Hammarskjold was skeptical that the scheme could be put into practice, but by the end of their meal Pearson had convinced him that the obstacles could be overcome. After a quick trip to Ottawa to report to the Prime Minister and Cabinet, Pearson returned to New York for the November 3 meeting of the General Assembly. Again Canadian officials canvassed the UN delegates from other countries to determine the degree of support that existed for Canada's proposal. They were encouraged to learn that President Nasser agreed with it in principle. Pearson had already discussed the proposal with John Foster Dulles, who was in agreement, and with officials of Britain and France, who urged their governments not to veto it. Pearson told delegates from nineteen Afro-Asian countries, who had prepared a resolution calling for an immediate end to the fighting, that he would support their resolution if they would support his. Later that evening, with the ground-work now carefully laid, Pearson rose and introduced the Canadian resolution: 'The General Assembly ... requests, as a matter of priority, the Secretary-General to submit to it within forty-eight hours a plan for the setting up, with the consent of the nations concerned, of an emergency international United Nations force to secure and supervise the cessation of hostilities.' The resolution was passed 57 to 0 (with 19 abstentions). As a result of Pearson's skilful behind-the-scenes negotiating, the basis for the United Nations Emergency Force had been laid.

It was now necessary to put the proposal into practice. After only a few hours' sleep, since the previous day's meeting had extended well into the morning, Pearson met with

Hammarskjold and other UN officials and delegates in the Secretary-General's office. Hammarskjold suggested that a Canadian, General E.L.M. Burns, be made commander of the emergency force. It was also agreed that, because of the attitude of most African and Asian countries, neither British nor French troops would serve on the UN force as Pearson had originally contemplated. Egypt, initially reluctant to allow UN forces on its soil, became less hesitant when Britain and France began parachuting troops into the canal zone on November 4. Pearson recommended that Canada provide a contingent to the emergency force, and on November 7 Prime Minister St Laurent announced that Canada would contribute a self-contained batallion. One minor problem—although a major annoyance from Canada's point of view—arose when President Nasser informed the Secretary-General that he did not wish Canadian troops to be stationed on Egyptian territory since they wore uniforms similar to those of the British forces that had just invaded the country. His suspicions that Canada was 'pro-British' in this UN endeavour would have been strengthened had he known that the Canadian batallion scheduled to be sent to Egypt was from the Queen's Own Rifles regiment. When Pearson learned of this, he asked whether any other unit was available. Wasn't there, he asked (only half-joking), something called the First East Kootenay Anti-Imperialist Regiment? After lengthy discussions between the UN secretariat and Egypt, General Burns suggested a compromise: Canada would provide administrative, transport, and medical personnel instead of an infantry batallion, which could be sent later if necessary. These specialist troops were badly needed if the UN force were to function effectively. Pearson, whose original reaction to Egypt's attitude had been one of considerable annoyance, was greatly relieved that Canada, who had proposed the creation of the force, would not be embarrassed by being excluded from it.

In the days that followed, Britain and France ordered their forces to cease fire, Israel withdrew its troops from the Sinai peninsula, and the Suez Canal was re-opened to traffic. The creation of the UN Emergency Force had brought, at least temporarily, peace to the Middle East.

This was the diplomatic triumph of Pearson's career. He had sensed the appropriate moment for introducing the resolution at the UN; had been able to convince Hammarskjold that the plan was practical; and above all had succeeded in winning the support of other nations through his diplomatic expertise and the personal contacts he had built up over the years. As a Canadian official later said: 'Mike was able to do it because he was well thought of by the Israelis, he had been President of the Assembly, he knew half of the Foreign Ministers by their first names, he had the support of the U.S., and the Egyptian Minister, Fawzi, could talk to him rationally.' Geoffrey Murray wrote that Pearson had had the good sense to work off his frustrations and annoyances—with Egyptian suspicion, Israeli pressure, British condescension, and American haste—in the privacy of the Drake Hotel, where he stayed while in New York, rather than in public. Most of Canada's newspapers recognized the extent of his achievement. The Vancouver *Province* praised his 'remarkable performance of diplomacy', and the Winnipeg *Free Press* stated that he had kept his head while all about him were losing theirs. Former British Prime Minister Harold Macmillan wrote in his memoirs that 'Britain owes much to Pearson,' who, with his 'ease, tolerance, clarity of thought and expression', resisted the joint American-Soviet pressure 'to inflict upon us humiliation as well as retreat.'

Much to Pearson's surprise, his great international success led to a political controversy at home that seriously weakened the St Laurent government. The Progressive Conservative party attacked the government for not fully supporting the actions of Britain and France. It considered Pearson's support of the Afro-Asian cease-fire resolution as a 'gratuitous condemnation' of the two mother countries. Many Canadians still felt an instinctive loyalty to Great Britain, for almost half the population was of British origin. A British publication described the Canadian reaction to the British invasion of Egypt as 'almost tearful . . . like finding a beloved uncle arrested for rape'. A Gallup Poll taken in Toronto showed that 43 per cent of those questioned approved of British and French policy in the Middle East (while 40 per cent did not). Prime Minister St Laurent did not help matters when he said in the House of Commons that he had been 'scandalized' more than once by the actions of the 'supermen of Europe' who did whatever they pleased. Pearson tried to show that his actions had been designed on the one hand to prevent a condemnation of Britain in the UN and to help Britain save face (as Macmillan later confirmed in his memoirs) and on the other to maintain the unity of the Commonwealth that had been endangered by the severe criticism of Britain expressed by Asian members such as India. But this explanation was overlooked by many Canadians whose emotions had been aroused by the Conservatives' appeal to their British loyalties. Pearson, convinced he had done the right thing, was disturbed by this criticism, which he regarded as unjust. He was distressed to see how, in the rough-and-tumble world of politics, appeals to the emotions could have more effect than well-reasoned arguments.

On June 10, 1957, Canadians went to the polls to choose

their next government. The Liberals, who had been in power since 1935, were confident of victory. But the Conservatives had a new and energetic leader, John Diefenbaker, whose humble origins and concern for the 'ordinary people' gave him a considerable populist appeal. He was a master orator, skilled at arousing his listeners' emotions. By comparison the Liberals appeared complacent and apathetic, the Prime Minister tired and listless. The most important election issue was the government's arrogance, the result of twenty-one uninterrupted years in office. Diefenbaker capitalized skilfully on the government's imposition of closure during parliamentary debate on the pipeline bill.* Resentment over Pearson's 'betrayal' of Britain also hurt the government, although this was not a major issue in many places except 'loyalist' Ontario. When the ballots were counted, the seemingly invincible St Laurent government had been defeated. The Conservatives won 112 seats, the Liberals 105. Pearson himself was re-elected easily in Algoma East, although his majority of 3,617 votes in the 1953 election fell to 2,817.

After having been Canada's internationally respected Secretary of State for External Affairs for almost ten years, Pearson suddenly found himself in the position of an ordinary Member of Parliament. His change in status was most noticeable when the new Parliament met in October 1957. Pearson no longer had his grand departmental office in the

---

* The government, committed to having a pipeline built to bring natural gas from Alberta to the markets of central Canada, imposed closure to cut off debate in the House in order to meet its tight schedule for concluding the financial arrangements. The Opposition's indignation was heightened by procedural errors committed by both the government and the Speaker.

Arnold Heeney recalled later that this was a wretched time for Pearson, who 'recoiled from many of the petty aspects of public life.' He was relieved to escape from the turmoil of the pipeline debate in March for a trip to Washington, where he went to a baseball game, 'his favourite form of relaxation'.

East Block (an office once occupied by Sir John A. Macdonald, just down the hall from Prime Minister St Laurent's
office), nor his comfortable House of Commons office in the
Centre Block of the Parliament Buildings. Instead he was
assigned a small basement office in the Centre Block.

On October 14 Mr Diefenbaker and his new ministers
were making last-minute preparations for the opening of the
new session of Parliament, which Queen Elizabeth II was to
attend, while Pearson spent the day getting installed in his
basement quarters. Pearson reflected gloomily that it was Mr
St Laurent who had originally invited the Queen to come to
Ottawa for the ceremonial opening. Suddenly the telephone
rang. The call was from a Canadian Press reporter who
asked: 'What comment do you have on winning the Nobel
Peace Prize?' Pearson said that he must simply have been
nominated for it. The reporter read him a telegram that left
no doubt that he had been awarded the prize. 'Gosh!' stam-
mered Pearson. 'I'll have to call my wife and let her know.'
That night, at a state dinner at the Governor General's residence in honour of the Queen, Her Majesty took Pearson
aside to compliment him on the honour—a euphoric end to
a day that had begun depressingly.

On December 11, 1957, Pearson received the award at a
ceremony in Oslo, Norway. The Nobel official in charge of
the presentation said that the award was being given 'not to
the politician or the Secretary of State as such, but to the
man, Lester Pearson, because of his personal qualities, his
powerful initiative, strength and perseverance displayed in
attempting to prevent or limit war operations and restore
peace.'

Pearson's acceptance speech was entitled 'The Four Faces of
Peace'. He began by saying that the Secretary-General of the
United Nations deserved credit for the actual organization of

After receiving the Nobel Peace Prize, Pearson is congratulated by Gunnar Jahn of the Nobel Committee, December 1957.

the UN force and that this undertaking was only a beginning from which he hoped a stable peace could be attained. He noted that this was the 'first genuinely international police force of its kind' and that it may have 'prevented a brush fire from becoming an all-consuming blaze.' He then turned to the 'four faces of peace': people, power, policy, and trade. 'In the end,' he said, 'the whole problem always returns to people'; increased contacts and understanding are necessary if people in different countries can no longer defend themselves by means of war and physical power, 'since total war is total destruction'. International agreements and defensive coalitions were needed to remove the causes of war. He pleaded for a more frank and complete exchange of views between countries, especially the U.S. and the U.S.S.R., since 'we prepare for war like precocious giants and for peace like retarded pygmies.' Pearson added that it was equally important for the cause of peace that the underdeveloped countries of the world be helped by the more fortunate. 'Above all,' he concluded, 'we must find out why men with generous and understanding hearts, and peaceful instincts in their normal individual behaviour, can become fighting and even savage national animals under the incitements of collective emotion.' He told the story of the Christmas eve he spent in London during the Second World War, when he turned on the radio to drown out the sound of an air raid. After fumbling with the dial he heard waves of glorious Christmas choral music and then the voice of the announcer . . . speaking in German. He had been listening to a German radio station. 'Nazi bombs screaming through the air with their message of war and death . . . German music drifting through the air with its message of peace and salvation. When we resolve the paradox of those two sounds from a single national source, we will, at last, be in a good position to understand and resolve the problem of peace and war.'

The Suez crisis of 1956 marked the zenith of Canadian

foreign policy and of Lester Pearson's international statesmanship. Canada's influence had been growing steadily since
the end of the Second World War, but not until Suez did
Canada gain wide acclaim for its contribution to world peace.
The London *Daily Telegraph* observed in 1957 that 'No
country has grown in international stature so swiftly and
markedly as Canada has done during the Middle-East crisis.
. . . Hers has often been a lonely voice of reason, crying in
the wilderness of fantasy, "expectations", and "assump-
tions".' Lester Pearson's leadership, plus a combination of
favourable external and domestic circumstances, had given
Canada a 'golden decade' in the field of foreign affairs, and
on the international stage he himself had reached the summit.

4

Leader of the Opposition

One day during the summer of 1957, Pearson received a telephone call from a member of Louis St Laurent's family. The caller said that the Liberal leader was in poor health, depressed over the election defeat, and anxious to retire, but that he hesitated to retire for fear he would 'let the party down'. Pearson was asked to visit his party leader and convince him that he should step down. He was at first reluctant, for he knew that he had been mentioned in the press as a possible successor to St Laurent and was afraid his visit might be interpreted as self-seeking on his part. After repeated urgings he finally agreed to go, but only on two conditions: that the visit be kept completely secret, and that he be accompanied by another former Cabinet minister, Lionel Chevrier. The two spent a day and a half with St Laurent at his summer retreat near Québec City and convinced him that, in view of the circumstances, he would not be regarded as a 'quitter' if he wished to give up the leadership. The former prime minister finally agreed, much to the relief of his family. Pearson and Chevrier undertook to draft the retirement announcement, but not before St Laurent had received an assurance from Pearson that he would allow his name to stand at the Liberal party's forthcoming leadership convention.

Pearson's decision to contest the leadership was, by his

own reckoning, the most difficult decision he had ever made. It was much harder than his original decision to enter politics in 1948, for then he was merely taking one further step up the External Affairs ladder—from under-secretary to secretary. He was going to be working in his field of expertise, and the Liberal party was at the height of its power. In 1957, however, the first task of a new leader would be to rebuild a crumbling party. Moreover, he would be plunged into the still-uncomfortable world of partisan politics. He could easily have found in some international organization a job that better suited his talents and inclinations, rather than running the risk of tarnishing his already considerable reputation by becoming involved in a potentially futile search for political power. Arnold Heeney observed during a visit to Ottawa that Pearson 'shrank from the sort of personal competition which other candidacies would involve.' If he had to stand for the leadership, 'he hoped that he would be offered the post unopposed', for he was hesitant to engage in the self-promotion that would otherwise be required.

Yet despite these considerations Pearson entered the race. He did so primarily because of a sense of duty towards the party. 'The pressure from my friends,' he later explained, 'was great and made me feel that, having entered the government and politics "at the top", I had no right to refuse to stand for the leadership if my name was put forward, especially in the less than favourable circumstances that faced the party.' Even though he had not acquired the style or inclinations of a professional politician, he was beginning to develop a real party loyalty (sometimes confused, in his own mind, with his loyalty to friends who were associated with the party).

There was little doubt from the beginning that Pearson was the favourite. His Nobel Peace Prize, which he had accepted formally in December, gave him enormous public appeal and prestige. Most of the Young Liberals were for him, although there were some 'old-guard' party members who regarded him as too much of a political amateur ever to be successful. His major opponent for the leadership was Paul Martin, a skilful politician who had been in the House of Commons since 1935. When Pearson announced his candidacy in December, Martin had already been busy for several months building his contacts (already considerable) within the party. Pearson ran his leadership campaign without leaving Ottawa. His natural aversion to political campaigning was in sharp contrast to the gregarious inclinations of Martin, who did not hesitate to go to the Ottawa railway station to shake the hands of arriving delegates. Yet, as the delegates gathered in the Ottawa Coliseum—decorated with bunting and large pictures of Laurier, King, and St Laurent and with the fragrance of a recent livestock show still in the air—it was clear that Pearson was the party's choice. There was little of the colour and excitement that marked later leadership campaigns in Canada—only a few University of Toronto students in sober business suits and girls in cashmere sweaters shouting 'Hurrah for Mike'. Pearson won handily on the first ballot, receiving 1,074 votes to Martin's 305. The 'amateur politician' had become leader of Her Majesty's Loyal Opposition.

In his acceptance speech, Pearson told the delegates: 'I'm quite sure that I'll make some mistakes, but if I do I can promise you they will be honest mistakes for which I won't have to apologize to my conscience'. As one writer later noted: 'He was more prophetic than he could have guessed.' It was not long before Pearson's worst fears were realized.

As the new Liberal leader, he first had to decide what

tactics he would use in the House of Commons. His personal inclination was to follow St Laurent's previous strategy and avoid trying to rally the support of the CCF and Social Credit to defeat the Diefenbaker government through a vote of non-confidence. He thought it would be politically unwise— as well as bad for the country—to force an election during the winter at a time when unemployment was high and a strong government was needed. Several of his advisers, however, thought that the Opposition should become more aggressive and should immediately move a non-confidence motion. They pointed out that the Conservatives had only seven more seats than the Liberals, and that the Liberals might be able to win enough support from the third parties in Parliament to defeat the government and force another election, in which they would regain power. Pearson's physical exhaustion (he had spent a hectic week preparing for the leadership convention and had gone two consecutive nights without sleep) made the decision all the more difficult.

Then Pearson received the advice that he finally accepted. It came from Jack Pickersgill, a Cabinet minister in the St Laurent government and one of the Liberal party's top 'back-room' strategists. He proposed a plan that would supposedly combine the best of both strategies: submit a motion for the government to resign, but not one that would force an election. If the motion carried, the Diefenbaker government would be ousted and the Governor General could invite Pearson to form a new government with the support of the CCF and Social Credit. Pearson was skeptical. He thought the suggestion was 'a bit too clever'. But eventually he accepted it, feeling that Pickersgill was much more experienced in politics than he was, and that his advice was therefore likely to be sound.

The House of Commons met at 2:30 p.m. on Monday, January 20. Pearson listened as Prime Minister Diefenbaker extended his regrets that Louis St Laurent's health had not permitted him to continue to head his party, and congratulated Pearson on his new position. Then came Question Period. As soon as it ended, Pearson rose to make his first speech as leader of the Liberal party. From the beginning he was on the offensive. 'The record of Tory achievement in seven months,' he said, was one of 'dismal failure'. He pointed to the high rate of unemployment, the decline in trade and investment, and the confusion surrounding the new NORAD defence agreement. Then he reached the key part of his speech: 'In view of all these things, Mr Speaker, it is our view that His Excellency's advisers should, in the interest of his House of Commons, submit their resignations. Honourable members will know that the motion which I propose to move . . . is not designed to bring on an immediate election. . . . ' In short, he was asking Diefenbaker to step aside and let him become Prime Minister without an election.

Prime Minister Diefenbaker could hardly believe his ears. With the debating skill acquired through years of political experience, he proceeded to cut Pearson's arguments to shreds. Were the Liberals afraid of an election? he asked. How could they possibly ask a government elected only a few months earlier to step aside and let them take over? 'The only reason that this amendment is worded as it is is that my honourable friends opposite quake when they think of what will happen if an election comes.' Then he turned to the Opposition charges that the government was mismanaging the economy. The Prime Minister produced a confidential report written for the government while the Liberals were still in power, which showed that the economic situation was beginning to deteriorate. 'This record', said Diefenbaker, 'was in the possession of each and every minister in the former government . . . They went ahead with the policy which could not but accelerate the forces that were bringing about a deflationary condition in Canada . . . I put it to the honourable members opposite—every one of them in the official opposition—that they hid the facts; they concealed the record; they did not let the Canadian people know what was taking place.' As he quoted line after line from the report, showing that Canada's economic problems had begun while the Liberals were still in power, the mood of the Liberal members became increasingly gloomy. When the CCF and Social Credit leaders said they could not possibly support a motion calling for the return to power of the former government, it was clear that the Liberals' timing and strategy had been completely wrong.

Pearson's first day as party leader had been a disaster. It made him look inept and incompetent and further lowered party morale. A few days later he remarked to a friend: 'I don't know whether I'll ever be any good as leader, but one thing is sure: no leader ever made a bigger mistake at the outset of his term.' His political inexperience had been exposed. As a CCF member later summarized the day:

It was a rather tragic scene we witnessed. We saw something that was not very pretty to behold: we saw a magnificent hatchet job done on the Liberal opposition in this House . . . And yet I wonder if that is the role which the Prime Minister of Canada should play . . . When I saw him bring whole batteries of guided missiles of vitriol and invective in order to shoot one forlorn sitting duck—a sitting duck, indeed, already crippled with a self-inflicted wound—I wondered if the Prime Minister believes in the humane slaughter of animals.

Pearson's misguided strategy gave Diefenbaker the opportunity he wanted to call an election. He had been seeking the right moment to appeal to the people for a majority government, and Pearson had given it to him. The Prime Minister dissolved Parliament and called an election for March 31, 1958.

Pearson's first national election campaign as party leader was also a disaster. Diefenbaker's most popular target was Pearson's January 20 motion in the House of Commons. Before audience after audience Diefenbaker would mimic Pearson: 'Put us back—but don't have an election.' Then he would add scornfully: 'Did you ever hear in the days when you used to play marbles and you won, that the other fellow said, "Give me back my marbles?" ' His listeners roared. Voters found it easy to agree with Diefenbaker that, if the Liberals really believed in tax reductions and stimulating the economy, they should have shown they did while they were in power. After all, he pointed out, his 'secret report' showed that they were aware of the problem. In reality Diefenbaker's accusations were not as valid as they appeared, for the report to which he referred was only one of many that had been prepared for the St Laurent government. Other departments had concluded that there was little danger of an economic recession, and it was on this majority view that the government of Louis St Laurent had acted. But such details mattered little to Diefenbaker. He had a good election issue and, like the experienced politician he was, he knew how to use it. Pearson, for his part, found it hard to forgive Diefenbaker for using this confidential document in such a way. It was the beginning of a long feud between the two men.

Pearson, the political amateur, was completely outshone by Diefenbaker, the practised professional. Diefenbaker was a master orator who could sway audiences with his rhetoric. He promised Canadians a 'Vision for Canada'—economic growth and northern development—but most of all he promised them leadership. 'A country starved of leadership for nearly half a century', wrote novelist Hugh MacLennan, 'had reached the point where it craved leadership more than anything.' Diefenbaker had wanted to be Prime Minister ever since the age of six, and was perfectly suited to appeal to the popular mood. Pearson, on the other hand, was reserved and shy. He found it difficult to walk up to strangers and shake their hand. And he found it impossible to deliver rousing, emotional speeches. He was too willing to see both sides of a position, and his diplomatic training had made him wary of the extremism and emotionalism that Diefenbaker used to great advantage. Diefenbaker, in short, was appealing to Canadians' emotions. Pearson was appealing to their reason, but in an uninspiring way. His proposals—a temporary tax reduction, improved social security measures, and a federal scholarship scheme—were economically sound, but it was difficult for most voters not to agree with John Diefenbaker when he said that if the Liberals really believed in the importance of these measures, they should have introduced them while they were in power. On top of everything, the Liberal party organization was weak and demoralized.

On election night Lester Pearson and his wife went to the Château Laurier in downtown Ottawa to eat oyster stew and watch the election results. 'The oysters were wonderful', Pearson remarked wryly to a friend later, but 'the TV show was about the worst I ever saw.' John Diefenbaker led the Progressive Conservatives to the largest majority government in Canadian history with 208 seats. Lester Pearson's Liberals fell from 105 seats to a mere 48. It was the Liberal party's worst electoral defeat since Confederation. As the results came in throughout the evening, there was no report from Pearson's own riding of Algoma East. Mrs Pearson, who had never liked politics, began to hope that her husband would lose his own seat since, on top of a defeat for the whole party, that might force him to leave political life for good. Late in the evening a red star, signifying a Liberal victory, was put up beside Algoma East on the board at Liberal Party Headquarters. A mild roar went up from party workers, who had had little to cheer about all night. For Mrs Pearson it was the ultimate disaster. Turning to her husband, she said: 'We've lost everything. We've even won our own seat.'

Since the Conservatives had just been given a clear mandate from the Canadian public, there was little the Opposition could do except let the government govern. In the House of Commons, Pearson applauded the government when he agreed with it instead of taking the view that the role of the Opposition was solely to oppose. He believed that his party's function was to scrutinize the government—to keep it on its toes so that it would not make mistakes. Not so with some of his colleagues. Paul Martin, Jack Pickersgill, and Lionel Chevrier were all old-style politicians whose instinct was to oppose the government at all times. They turned the daily Question Period in the House of Commons into a full-scale battle, trying to embarrass the government rather than asking questions solely to obtain information. It was not long before journalists began writing that they were trying to force the government to call an election by obstructing the business of Parliament. Aside from these three, and Pearson (soon referred to in the press as the 'Four Horsemen'), the Liberal members of the Opposition were for the most part a sorry lot. Many of the best Liberals had been defeated in the 1958 election. Judy LaMarsh, a Liberal elected in a 1960 by-election, gave this description of the Liberal MPs whom she met when she arrived in Ottawa: 'Hopeless, apathetic, drinking too much and working too little, very few of the 49 (I became number 50) were paying any attention to the growing public disillusionment with the Diefenbaker adminis-tration.' Pearson and his front-benchers were working hard, but the party was demoralized.

With little opportunity for constructive activity in the House of Commons, Pearson had ample time to speak to outside groups. He had always been popular among intellec-tuals and young people, and was frequently asked to speak at universities and clubs. At some of these meetings he philoso-phized about the role of the Opposition. Opposition politi-cians, he said, were 'detergents of democracy' whose job was to 'cleanse and purify those in office'. The good Opposition leader 'doesn't go around looking for belts so that he may hit below them, or, on the other hand, looking for a parade merely so that he may lead it.' (Such comments provoked a retort by politician Pickersgill that Pearson's trouble was that 'he wanted to solve the government's problems for them'.)

Freed from the responsibility of office, Pearson also had the time to participate in the kind of international activities that he particularly enjoyed. In 1959 he was asked to become chairman of the Council on World Tensions, which met periodically in various parts of the world to examine interna-tional problems. Such meetings gave him the opportunity to talk about the 'two great gaps in our world' that greatly concerned him. There was a gap between moral and material progress, he believed, for in spite of man's scientific genius he had not learned how to live in peace with his neighbours; and there was a gap between poor and rich countries, which threatened to create tensions that could destroy the world. No matter how embroiled he became in domestic politics, he could not forget the larger issues of world peace and security.

Much of Pearson's time was taken up with meeting his parliamentary colleagues and attending to the assorted administrative tasks expected of a party leader. His talent for dealing with people served him well in these duties. Lionel Chevrier wrote later: 'I doubt if there was any other period of his life when Mike Pearson's diplomacy was more constantly needed or employed to better effect. In caucus, in meetings of the "shadow" cabinet, and in private conversations with him, every member of the party was always sure of a sympathetic hearing. He was patient, kind, and generous.'

Pearson was the prime target for his political opponents, however. The vilification that he received constantly from the Conservatives, and especially from John Diefenbaker, was beginning to get to him. Some of his colleagues wondered whether he would be able to endure much longer the provocation to which he was subjected almost daily in the House and the frequent press criticism that is the lot of almost any party leader. There were times when Pearson longed for the relative tranquillity of an international position, in which he knew he would feel comfortable. After much soul-searching he returned one day after a long weekend and told Chevrier: 'I have given a lot of thought in the last few days to my position as Leader of the Opposition. I have decided to stick to the job. I do not care what Diefenbaker says about me. I intend to ignore him completely and go about my duties as efficiently as I can.'

This decision coincided with a change in Pearson's attitude to his objectives. During his first two years as Opposition leader he was content to co-operate frequently with the government in improving legislation and, when desirable, in

smoothing its path through the House of Commons, in keeping with his belief that an Opposition should be constructive,
not negative. But by 1960 his attitude began to change. The
government seemed to him to be increasingly incompetent.
He had given it a chance to govern, but its actions convinced
him that it was undermining the well-being of the country.
The Canadian economy was in the midst of one of the most
serious recessions since the great Depression of the 1930s,
and the government seemed incapable of deciding upon any
constructive measures. Above all, Pearson had developed an
intense personal aversion to John Diefenbaker. Diefenbaker's
tendency to over-simplify issues, to destroy rational argument
by a rhetorical appeal to his listeners' emotions, as well as
his egotism and indecision, had convinced Pearson that he
must defeat the Prime Minister at all costs. This determination was exactly what was needed to make Pearson act as a
politician. Without this conviction that he had a duty to
perform, he could not launch an all-out attack against the
Conservatives. Now, his conscience clear, he could direct his
energy towards ousting the government.

The first essential step was to rebuild the Liberal party
organization, which had been shattered after the defeats of
1957 and 1958. Pearson began talking with his closest
friends: Walter Gordon, an accountant and economic adviser
with whom he had worked on Royal Commissions during the
1930s; Maurice Lamontagne, an economist and professor;
Robert Fowler, president of the Canadian Pulp and Paper
Association; and Tom Kent, a newspaperman. After the
disastrous advice he had already received from politicians like
Jack Pickersgill, Pearson was turning to the kind of people
with whom he felt most at ease. The idea gradually emerged
that new life could be injected into the party through a full-

scale re-examination of its philosophy. This would attract new
young minds to the party, would give it the appearance of
vigour, and would arouse considerable public attention. Pearson was personally interested in orienting the party towards the
left. He felt instinctively that it was failing to reflect new ideas
that were present in Canadian society. Increasing urbanization
brought with it the need for improved social policy; economic
problems cried out for new solutions; and Canada's worsening
relations with the United States raised the question of Canada's proper role in the world.

Pearson asked Mitchell Sharp, a former senior civil servant
who had resigned after the 1958 election, to organize a
conference of interested Canadians to discuss what the policies of a liberal Canadian political party should be. He
encouraged him to invite people who were not members of
the Liberal party. Sharp asked several of Canada's brightest
thinkers to a conference that convened at Queen's University
in Kingston on September 6, 1960. There they discussed
ideas as diverse as free trade with the United States, the
acquisition of nuclear weapons by Canada, and the need for
tax incentives to encourage investment in the country. The
Toronto *Globe and Mail* sarcastically referred to the meeting
as 'an egghead conference', and said that Mr Pearson, 'something of an egghead himself', was too engrossed in ideas ever
to achieve results. In Pearson's opinion, however, the Kingston Conference was the 'beginning of our comeback'. William Kilbourn later wrote: 'As a means of finding policies,
his Kingston Conference in 1960 may possibly have been the
idle, ivory-tower occupation for which it was mocked by the
Globe and Mail. But as a political symbol to attract a
variety of thoughful Canadians and as the unintended instru-

ment for finding workers and candidates for the next two elections, it was an unqualified success.'

The next step was to organize a national party convention, which was held in Ottawa in January 1961. Having received the views of a wide variety of Canadians, Pearson wanted to see what Liberal party members thought about certain issues. Some important new policies were proposed and eventually incorporated into the party platform, but the main achievement was a great increase in party morale. Members now felt that the party was alive again and that it knew where it was going. So did Pearson. The size and enthusiasm of the rally greatly encouraged him and lifted his spirits. He sensed a new feeling of optimism within the party that the Diefenbaker government could be defeated.

The third vital step was to rebuild the party's electoral machinery. Pearson turned this task over to Walter Gordon and Lionel Chevrier. The two campaign managers began to organize the party in the various constituencies across the country, finding people who would work for it during the next election. Gordon also began recruiting people to serve on Pearson's personal staff so that he could be assured of good advice. Maurice Lamontagne became his economic consultant, Tom Kent a speechwriter, Richard O'Hagan his press adviser. All were to play key roles when Pearson finally became Prime Minister.

When the Diefenbaker government swept the country in the 1958 election, observers believed that it was destined to stay in office for many years to come. Not only had the Liberal party been destroyed, but the Conservatives had an appealing new leader and an image of a new Canada that they would build. Canadians were willing to place their trust in the government. No matter how well Lester Pearson rebuilt his party organization, he would have little success unless something happened to lessen this sense of confidence in the Diefenbaker administration. As Pearson, a student of history, well knew, when governments fall it is usually because of their own weaknesses rather than the strength of the Opposition.

The event that provided the first major indication of a fatal weakness within the Diefenbaker government was the 'Coyne affair' of 1961. James Coyne was the Governor of the Bank of Canada. He felt that the government's expansive monetary policies were having a harmful effect on the country's economy, and said so publicly in a series of speeches across Canada, much to the embarrassment of the government. Before long the Diefenbaker administration asked for his resignation. But Coyne refused to resign and demanded that he be allowed to appear before a parliamentary committee to defend his economic views and his integrity.

The strategists in the Liberal party quickly realized that this was the opportunity to embarrass the government that they had been waiting for. Pearson, however, remained in control of the situation and refused to let himself be carried to extremes. He realized that he could not publicly support Coyne's economic views, for he did not believe in a restrictive monetary policy during a period of high unemployment any more than did the government. But the government's refusal to allow Coyne to defend himself before a committee provided Pearson with a perfect weapon. He stressed that Coyne should not be denied his 'day in court' and was entitled to the democratic right of having a hearing before he was judged, just like any other citizen. Since the Liberals still dominated the Senate, they were able to arrange a Senate committee meeting at which Coyne set out his complaints against the government. Feeling he had made his point, Coyne then resigned.

The Coyne affair was a turning-point in Pearson's political career. The government had been badly embarrassed by the controversy. For the first time Pearson began to think that the Diefenbaker administration was not as impregnable as it had first appeared and that the Liberals had a real chance to regain power. He came to see the role of the Opposition in a new light. It was not only a means for keeping the government on its toes but also an instrument for arousing public discontent against the government and for eventually overthrowing it. His interest in political organization increased and he urged Gordon and Chevrier to continue their efforts to rebuild the party at the grass roots.

By 1962 a sense of disillusionment with the Diefenbaker government had spread across much of the country. The Utopia that Diefenbaker promised in 1958 had not come to pass. Instead there were four long winters of rising unemployment. Canada's relations with the United States had deteriorated, in large part because of a personality clash between Prime Minister Diefenbaker and President Kennedy, and Canada's reputation among other countries was plummeting because of its unrealistic foreign policy. The opinion polls gave proof of this change in the public's attitude towards Diefenbaker. In a 1958 survey the Conservatives were favoured by 60 per cent of Canadians, compared to 30 per cent who supported the Liberals; but by 1962 the Liberals had moved ahead of the Conservatives in popularity by a margin of 45 per cent to 38 per cent.

In April 1962 Prime Minister Diefenbaker announced that a general election would be held on June 18. Despite the Liberals' growing popularity, he hoped to win the election by accusing them of obstructing the work of Parliament. Above all he was confident that he would be able to out-campaign Lester Pearson and regain on the hustings the popularity his government had lost in Parliament.

The Liberals proved the adage that elections are lost, not won. They waged a weak campaign and their ideas seemed confused to many voters. On the one hand Pearson called for more responsible financial management, while on the other he promised major social reforms that would have necessitated heavy government spending. Above all Pearson was unable to communicate with the voters. The Liberal party strategists tried everything in an attempt to improve his public image. They hired a voice coach and enlisted the services of the MacLaren Advertising Agency—but to no avail. No matter how warm and witty Pearson was in small groups, his reserve in public made him appear cold and indecisive. On one occasion his advisers urged him to go and eat with unemployed men in a mission-house where he could be photographed, but Pearson refused. 'I just can't exploit their misery for politics,' he said. This reaction showed the extent of his compassion and his humanitarianism, but it also showed that he was incapable of making the calculated gestures that are often necessary for political success. Mrs Pearson disliked political campaigning as much as, if not more than, her husband, and made no attempt to hide her feelings. After one strenuous day of receptions and meetings, she was asked at a gathering whether there was anything she would like to bring up before she left. 'Yes,' replied Mrs Pearson, 'the last five cups of coffee.'

Diefenbaker for his part campaigned aggressively, but without the flair or imagination he had shown in 1958. He devoted a large portion of his time to ridiculing Pearson's advisers. He called Walter Gordon 'the Toronto taxidermist who fills Mr Pearson with flossy economic ideas'; Mitchell Sharp was 'the man whose favourite sport is pushing people around and breaking the law'; Tom Kent was 'a dreamer and philosophic socialist who wants to tax advertising.' These repeated insults appeared to many Canadians to be nothing more than crude attempts to make fun of educated men. It was an attitude that might win votes in some rural areas, but it lost the Conservatives prestige and credibility in most parts of the country.

When the ballots were counted on June 18, the Conservatives still formed the government, but just barely. Their strength in Parliament dropped from 208 seats to 116. The Liberals more than doubled their representation, from 48 seats to 99. In fact Pearson would probably have won despite his ineffective campaign had it not been for two factors: the Social Credit party surprised everyone by winning 26 seats in Québec, many of which might otherwise have gone to the Liberals; and the way in which the electoral boundaries were drawn tended to favour rural ridings, which the Conservatives dominated. However, this rural strength was soon to spell their doom. The trend towards urbanization was increasing and by 1962 more than half the country's population lived in fifteen metropolitan centres. The election results showed clearly that the Conservatives had lost strength in these areas. Of 58 seats in Montreal, Toronto, Ottawa, Winnipeg, and Vancouver, the Conservatives won only nine. The Diefenbaker government, increasingly indecisive and divided, no longer stood for the kind of progressive policies urban Canadians wanted. The Liberals, on the other hand, had shifted their philosophy to the left after the Kingston conference and, with a leader who appealed more to reason than to emotion, were in a better position to capitalize on the trend towards urbanization.

Pearson was therefore not too despondent as he watched

the results on television in the two-storey brick building that served as headquarters for the National Liberal Federation. The Conservatives had after all been reduced to a minority government and had lost more seats than any other Canadian government in history. The Liberals had more than doubled their representation—no mean feat for a party that many thought was dead after 1958. Pearson's most pressing thought at the time, though, was that the results showed he would soon have to go through the whole process again—and another election campaign was the last thing he wanted. But the Liberals had not been decisively beaten (he would have been obliged to retire if they had been) and it was doubtful that the Diefenbaker government could survive for long, especially in a minority situation. 'Therefore,' Pearson later reflected, 'there was no alternative but to go through it again. The prospect didn't cause me any great delight, but I thought, "the sooner the better", to get this over with.'

Only six days after the election the Diefenbaker government shocked the country by introducing an austerity program that cut government spending, increased the duty on imports, and restricted the duty-free exemptions allowed to Canadians travelling abroad. The economy was obviously in serious trouble despite the government's claims during the election campaign that all was well. Pearson's political advisers urged him to denounce the government for having 'deceived the people', but Pearson had learned to be wary of political advice. He let himself be guided this time by his diplomatic instinct, which told him that if he attacked the government he could be accused—perhaps justifiably—of hindering its attempts to solve a serious national problem. He was convinced that the government was weak and would soon disintegrate as long as he did not give it the ammunition with which to forge an election issue.

However, when Parliament met on September 27, 1962,

the Liberals immediately began to press for an election. The government had been particularly indecisive during the summer, partly because the Prime Minister was confined to bed for several weeks with a broken ankle and a severe case of depression. Speaking during the debate on the Speech from the Throne, Pearson said: 'We feel it is not only our duty but our privilege to move a vote of non-confidence so that this House may decide whether it wishes the Government to carry on, or whether it wishes the people to be given a chance to put into office a government which will know how to carry on.' The government managed to gain enough support from the third parties to survive for the time being but was able to accomplish little. Only eight items of the thirty-four mentioned in the Speech from the Throne were passed. Consideration of the spending estimates fell far behind schedule, and there was no sign of a budget. Nevertheless the government managed to hold onto its majority in the House and thwart the efforts of the Liberals to force an election.

Pearson soon decided that it was time for him to take the offensive and to begin offering concrete policy alternatives to those of the Conservatives. One of the most significant speeches of his career was made in the House of Commons on December 17, 1962, when he proposed a new role for French Canada within the Canadian Confederation. Since the beginning of the 'quiet revolution' in 1960, Québec had sought to reform and modernize its institutions. The provincial government, which had taken over control of educational and health and welfare institutions from the Church, needed more money from Ottawa if it was to continue its reforms. In addition, French Canadians wanted to share in the running of major institutions in which they had previously held only secondary positions—especially the federal government, where French-Canadian ministers usually held minor Cabinet portfolios and where French-speaking civil servants were required to work almost entirely in English if they wished to advance. The Diefenbaker government had been insensitive to the new spirit of progress in Québec. It seemed to think that by providing simultaneous-interpretation facilities in the House of Commons and bilingual government cheques it was meeting the aspirations of French Canada. Nothing could have been further from the truth. Québec had thrown off its traditional antipathy towards the Conservatives in 1958, but four years later the respected Montreal newspaper editor André Laurendeau complained that 'Not since the days of R. B. Bennett have French Canadians felt themselves so absent from the affairs of state, as under Mr Diefenbaker.' French Canadians received no major portfolios in the Diefenbaker government. The seeds of nationalism and separatism were sprouting in Québec. Many felt that if Quebeckers could not play an equal role with English Canadians in Ottawa, why should they not form an independent state of Québec in which French Canadians could make their voices heard?

This was the sentiment that Pearson thought Diefenbaker was encouraging and that had to be stopped before it destroyed the country. Pearson was not familiar enough with Québec to know exactly what should be done, but his sense of fair play told him that changes had to be made. In his December 17 speech Pearson stressed that 'full participation in the discharge of national responsibilities along with the full enjoyment of rights and opportunities' for all French Canadians were essential for the survival of Canada. The answer, he said, depended primarily on English-speaking Canadians, who held the majority of positions in industry and the public service:

Are we willing to do it? Are we prepared not only to accept those long-term objectives of partnership but, perhaps more important and more difficult for us, to take immediate and concrete steps to achieve them? If the answer to these questions is in the affirmative, then we can be confident of the future of our united country. . . . But if the answer is negative, not so much the answer in words but the answer in fact, and if we become unaware or careless of the obligations and opportunities of true partnership, we will continue in this country to drift from one difficulty to another until a majority of people on both sides will have had enough of this unique Canadian experience. The final result of that would, indeed, be separatism.

In addition to stating his objective of full partnership, Pearson proposed the establishment of a commission to 'review the bicultural and bilingual situation in our country; our experiences in the teaching of English and French, and in the relations existing generally between our two founding racial groups.' This was the origin of the Royal Commission on Bilingualism and Biculturalism, established after Pearson became Prime Minister, which provided the detailed guidelines for French Canada's attainment of equal status. Pearson's speech was a spectacular success. It scored politically, showing Québec that only the Liberal party had a concept of its role in Confederation that could meet the aspirations growing out of the 'quiet revolution'. It' also appealed to many English Canadians' sense of fairness and added to the growing impression that the Liberal party was the one with new and progressive ideas. Pearson was to a certain extent groping for the best policy, placing his faith in French-Canadian advisers whose judgement he trusted, but he at least realized the general direction in which he wanted the party, and the country, to move.

Pearson's other main initiative was in the field of defence policy. It was sparked by the Cuban missile crisis of October 1962, when the discovery that the Soviet Union was placing offensive missiles on Cuba brought the United States and the U.S.S.R. to the brink of nuclear war. President Kennedy imposed a naval blockade on Cuba to prevent delivery of the missiles and called on his allies for support. Although most of the countries of Western Europe and Latin America responded promptly to the request for allied solidarity, Canada did not. Prime Minister Diefenbaker delayed placing Canada's armed forces on a state of alert for forty-two hours, and waited a day longer before stating publicly that Canada was standing by its ally. Pearson, who avoided criticizing the government publicly because of the seriousness of the crisis was deeply disappointed in Canada's response. The crisis proved, he felt, that in times of emergency Canada could not fail to become involved in American defence policy without seriously weakening the Western alliance that was necessary to ensure world peace. The government's delay—caused by Diefenbaker's indecision, his sensitivity to any U.S. domination of Canada, and his poor personal relations with President Kennedy—was also resented by many Canadians, including a considerable number of Conservatives. It was one more step on the government's road to defeat.

Most serious of all for the government was the issue, highlighted by the missile crisis, of whether Canada should possess nuclear weapons. The Diefenbaker government had purchased various missiles and aircraft which, without nuclear weapons, were virtually useless. But the Prime Minister delayed making the actual decision to acquire the warheads. He said that the government would do so only when grave international tensions indicated they might be needed. However, the Cuban missile crisis demonstrated that such a policy was not practical. In the first place there would not be enough time to install the nuclear warheads once a crisis arose; and in the second place such an action would probably be interpreted by the enemy as a provocative and hostile act and would only increase world tensions. Since the Cuban missile crisis had raised cold-war tensions to their highest point in years, there was considerable anxiety in Canada that the government was failing to take adequate steps to ensure the country's security and to contribute to world peace. Some Canadians built bomb shelters in their basements in the hope that this would protect them from the war that might come any day, and air-raid sirens were erected in most major cities to warn the population of a coming attack.

Pearson's own attitude to nuclear weapons had been mixed. He had long been opposed to having nuclear weapons on Canadian soil unless it could be demonstrated that they would make a decisive difference in continental defence, but he was prepared to accept them for Canada's forces in Europe if the U.S. surrendered control over them to NATO. The Liberal party, however, was opposed to Canada's possession of nuclear weapons under any condition. At their 1961 convention, delegates passed a resolution saying that Canada should not acquire or use nuclear weapons and that it should abandon its interception role in North American air defence.

The Cuban missile crisis gave Pearson second thoughts. As he later explained: 'It was the Cuban thing, more than anything else, that changed my mind. It was the thought that here we were, a part of continental defence, on the eve of this possible great tragedy, and we were completely impotent. Sentimentally I felt I was operating against my instincts in the past, which were that we should not have anything to do with these things [nuclear weapons].' As well, he was influenced by a report from his parliamentary colleague, Paul Hellyer, who had returned from a trip to Europe with the news that the government's failure to meet its military commitments was harming its reputation among Canada's allies and causing the morale of Canada's armed forces to deteriorate. Pearson was encouraged by the prospects for political gain when a Gallup Poll indicated that Canadians favoured the acquisition of nuclear weapons by a margin of 54 per cent to 32 per cent. However, he also realized that a change in Liberal policy would produce bitter recriminations, especially in Québec.

Pearson tried to reconcile his conflicting thoughts while he attended a conference on world tensions in New York. Pacing his room at the Sheraton-East Hotel one night, he finally made his decision, which he determined to work into a speech he was to deliver to a Liberal Association meeting in Toronto three days later, on January 12. After six drafts, the last of which he wrote in a Toronto hotel, his dramatic speech was ready.

Pearson reminded his audience that Canada's security depended on the nuclear deterrent provided by the United States, and that the government had agreed to participate in this system of collective security. 'As a Canadian,' he said, 'I am ashamed if we accept commitments and then refuse to discharge them. In acting thus, we deceive ourselves, we let our armed forces down, and betray our allies. As I understand international affairs, and I think it is the understanding of all Canadians, when you make, and continue to accept, commitments, you carry them out. If we had not done so in the past, Canada would not have achieved a position of respect and influence in the world.' He qualified his stand somewhat by saying that a Liberal government would discuss with the United States a 'more realistic and effective' defence role for Canada to play than one based on nuclear weapons, for he realized the need to appeal to the large segment of the Canadian public that (like himself) was emotionally repelled by the idea of Canada's possessing nuclear arms. Nevertheless his main message came out loud and clear: a Liberal government would fulfil Canada's obligations and accept nuclear weapons. According to his daughter, Pearson's decision to take this stand was the most difficult one he had ever made and caused him great personal anguish.

As he had anticipated, his speech resulted in furious accusations that he had abandoned his earlier principles. A Toronto group demanded that the Nobel Peace Prize Committee cancel its award to Pearson. Three former Liberal candidates announced they were shifting their party allegiance; the Québec intellectual, Pierre Elliott Trudeau, denounced him as 'the unfrocked prince of peace'; and the NDP Youth Council complained that, 'In his indecent haste to become prime minister, Mr Pearson is ready to abandon what people had hoped were his fundamental principles.' The Voice of Women, an outspoken pacifist organization, delivered such a bitter condemnation of the switch in policy that Mrs Pearson felt compelled to resign as the organization's honorary sponsor. However, despite the intense criticism his decision provoked, there were other indications that many Canadians agreed with him. Most newspaper editorials, including some in traditionally Conservative papers, supported his action, as did the Quebec Liberal Federation. Although many intellectuals were infuriated, Pearson seemed to have reflected the mood of the general public. And by insisting that Canada

Prime Minister and Mrs Pearson and John Diefenbaker at a garden party in honour of Queen Elizabeth, Ottawa, July 1967.

had to meet its commitments, rather than talking of nuclear weapons as desirable in themselves, he struck a responsive note in many Canadians. His diplomatic skills helped him pull off a major reversal of previous Liberal policy that could have spelled disaster for a less skilled tactician.

The defence issue, coming on top of all its other problems, broke the back of the Diefenbaker government. Defence Minister Douglas Harkness had been assured all along by the Prime Minister that the government was on the verge of acquiring nuclear warheads from the United States, but on January 30, 1963, the U.S. State Department revealed that, while discussions of an 'exploratory' nature had begun, the Canadian government 'has not as yet proposed any arrangement sufficiently practical to contribute effectively to North American defense.' Harkness resigned in exasperation. The resignation of the high-principled Defence Minister was the first clear sign of the dissension building up within the Diefenbaker Cabinet. Furthermore, the Social Credit party, on whom the minority Diefenbaker government had counted for support since the 1962 election, felt it could no longer tolerate the government's indecision and lack of action. Feeling the time was ripe to launch an attack on the government's performance, Pearson rose in the House on February 4 and, for more than an hour, delivered a scathing condemnation. He concluded by moving 'that this Government, because of lack of leadership, the breakdown of unity in the Cabinet, and confusion and indecision in dealing with national and international problems, does not have the confidence of the Canadian people.' This was a non-confidence motion that, if passed, would bring about the fall of the government. After the supper recess, having received no indication of any change in policy from

Diefenbaker, Robert Thompson, the Social Credit leader, introduced an amendment to the Pearson resolution that also condemned the government.

When the House of Commons met the next day, the public galleries were jammed by curious Ottawans who wanted to witness the decisive vote. Would the Prime Minister be able to arouse enough support among the opposition parties to stave off defeat? Fifteen hundred members of the public who had been unable to gain entry to the galleries waited expectantly in the Hall of Honour and rotunda of the Parliament Buildings. The House itself was unusually full as the party whips tried to ensure that every member was there to vote. The suspense was dispelled when Robert Thompson rose to his feet to record his party's vote in favour of his motion condemning the government. The Liberal members roared their approval and banged the lids of their desks in applause. Now it was clear that there would be enough votes to bring down the government. Pearson then rose to record his support of the amendment, and the rest of his party followed. Finally all but three members of the New Democratic Party followed suit as the Liberal backbenchers applauded wildly. There was then a vote on Pearson's original motion, and the result was the same: 142 in favour, 111 opposed. As the Clerk of the House announced the final count, pandemonium broke out on the floor. Liberal MPs flung their papers in the air in jubilation. Their shouts and cheers almost drowned out the Speaker's statement: 'I declare the amendment as amended carried.' The government had fallen. The noise subsided only when the Prime Minister rose. 'Mr Speaker,' declared John Diefenbaker, 'I shall advise His Excellency the Governor General tomorrow.' It was only the second time in Canadian history that a government had been defeated on a vote in the House of Commons. The election that Pearson and the Liberals wanted was about to take place.

As the campaign opened, the Liberals sought to take advantage of the excellent situation in which they found themselves. The government was badly divided and had suffered the extreme embarrassment of having been defeated in the House of Commons. Realizing that Pearson was no match for Diefenbaker as a campaigner, the party organizers tried to emphasize his decisiveness in contrast to the indecision that had come to characterize the Diefenbaker administration. At one point someone suggested that Pearson should propose a 'glorious 100 days of decision', until Mrs Pearson wisely reminded the organizers that a similar interval had destroyed Napoleon. Diefenbaker would be sure to seize the connection and use it to ridicule the Liberals. The slogan was therefore changed to '60 days of decision'. Speaking in Hamilton on March 25, Pearson promised that 'More constructive things will be done in the first sixty days of a new Liberal Government than in any similar period of Canadian history.' During the two weeks prior to the election, he made twenty-one specific policy pledges for the first sixty days. He would meet the leaders of the United States and Great Britain to restore harmonious relations, establish a Royal Commission on bilingualism and biculturalism, establish a $2-per-bushel floor price on wheat, bring in a budget, establish a municipal loan development board, create a contributory old-age pension scheme—all in the first sixty days of his government. To many Canadians it was, in the words of one commentator, 'a dazzling promise to a country heartily sick of equivocating'. Some realized, however, that by allowing his campaign to be dominated by a slogan—and especially one that could never be put into practice—Pearson was weakening his reputation as a serious statesman who was above politics, a reputation that his advisers had originally hoped to promote and that was a better reflection of the real man. The Vancouver *Province's* reaction was probably not shared by a majority of Canadians, but a significant number undoubtedly agreed with its criticism:

Now . . . a new Mike Pearson has emerged. Apparently he has been told to try all the old tricks. He has become a typical politician, an opportunist, a kisser of babies, the recipient of Indian headdresses and the promiser of all sorts of goodies for electors who vote for him . . . A good deal of this is inescapable . . . But in Pearson's case the Liberals are over-doing the act— obscuring the real Mike Pearson, a Canadian whose record shines with more real integrity and achievement than can be ever manufactured for him in the current popularity contest . . . If this is the best the Liberal braintrusters can do with such distinctive material, Mr Pearson should boot them out. He may have needed some political recasting, but it has been sadly overdone.

Nevertheless the Liberal campaign was a fairly effective one. In Québec Pearson's pledge to promote the 'duality of language and culture' in Canada helped win back votes that had gone to the Conservatives and Social Credit in 1958 and 1962. In Halifax he spoke eloquently of his desire to serve his country, not to gain power for its own sake. It was a line often used by politicians of all kinds, but at that meeting members of his audience began to rise spontaneously and applaud in a rare display of emotion for the obvious sincerity and humility of the man. A few instances such as this showed people responding enthusiastically to the real Pearson. But unfortunately for the Liberals, they were frustratingly infrequent.

Prime Minister Diefenbaker, on the other hand, tried to revive the mystic bond between himself and the 'average Canadian' that had been so strong in 1958. 'Everyone is against me but the people,' was his cry across the country. The United States provided him with a potentially potent campaign issue when the American Secretary of Defense told a Congressional committee that Bomarc missiles, which Canada had purchased from the United States, were little more than decoys. Why, charged Diefenbaker, does Pearson want to import nuclear warheads for these weapons if they are really useless? But many Canadians were more inclined to blame the Diefenbaker government for acquiring these 'useless' missiles in the first place. Diefenbaker seemed determined to wage an obliquely anti-American campaign. He attacked the Liberals for using the services of an American analyst who had worked on President Kennedy's campaign, saying that this proved the American government was working with the Liberals to have him defeated. He even pointed to a 1962 dinner arranged by the American government in honour of all North American winners of Nobel Prizes, to which Pearson was naturally invited, as further proof of the 'favoured' treatment given Pearson by the Kennedy administration.

Pearson for his part considered Diefenbaker's animosity towards the U.S. government to be sheer madness. But he knew that, for political reasons, he could not appear to side with an American president against a Canadian prime minister, and so he could only insist in his public statements that the two neighbours should end their disagreement. The United States, he said, was like a wife with whom a Canadian husband could not live easily and without whom he could not live at all. For the most part his appeal was successful, for the majority of Canadians also wanted their country to have good relations with the U.S. But the nuclear-weapons issue provided him with some uncomfortable moments during the campaign. Outside the Hamilton Forum his effigy was stoned by demonstrators protesting his decision to accept nuclear weapons. In Kingston he was howled into silence by an unruly audience and in Vancouver police dogs had to be used to keep back a surging crowd.

The rally in Vancouver, as the campaign neared its end, was a particular nightmare. An unruly demonstration outside the auditorium by opponents of Pearson's nuclear policy was matched by an equally noisy and antagonistic crowd inside. Pearson, filled with antibiotics for an infection, was not in the best of spirits to begin with. As he tried to speak, a couple of people in the balcony with peashooters kept bouncing their missiles off Pearson's head. The heckling was intense and nasty and Mrs Pearson was in tears as she watched her husband trying to defend himself. But Pearson refused to be intimidated. Instead of giving in to the hecklers he stood firm and matched them shout for shout. After the meeting drew mercifully to a close, Pearson complained to a Vancouver party organizer that it had been a disaster. On the contrary, said the organizer. It was a great victory and the party would probably gain seats because of the courage Pearson showed that night. 'Pearson flew east the next day,' wrote Bruce Hutchison, 'accompanied by his new legend of courage, to end the campaign in a crescendo of vigour, confidence, and righteous anger.' His dauntless behaviour in

Vancouver had indeed won him considerable public sympathy.

On March 30, nine days before the election, Canada's most prestigious newspaper, the Toronto *Globe and Mail*, ended its long-time support of the Conservative party and told its readers why it favoured the Liberals:

Mr Pearson is not a good speaker; he does not know how to indulge in dramatics or play the demagogue. But he is a sound, intelligent, honest man, who knows how to recruit good men and persuade them to work constructively together. His words from election podiums may not inspire Canadians; but his actions in world crises have inspired the world. They could well do the same in Canada's crisis.

We have had a man of words who was not a man of action. He has brought Canada into one of the most troubled and dangerous periods of her history, left us awash in a sea of indecision.

It is time for a change.

The reaction of the *Globe and Mail* and other traditionally Conservative newspapers that switched their support to the Liberals indicated that, if Canadians voted Liberal on April 8, they would be voting more *against* John Diefenbaker than *for* Lester Pearson. Although Pearson had waged an effective campaign that established him, as the *Globe and Mail* recognized, as a credible alternative, he had not captured the imagination of the public as Diefenbaker had in 1958 with his 'Vision of the North'. In fact Liberal support even declined in strength in the course of the campaign. Public-opinion polls showed that the Liberals were more popular just prior to the beginning of the campaign than they were on voting day. Many Canadians had been offended by cheap election gimmicks thought up by the Liberal organizers. The party published a child's colouring book filled with pictures ridiculing Diefenbaker and established a 'truth squad' to follow him across the country and point out the inaccuracies in his speeches. Many voters were appalled by the bad taste of the colouring book, and Diefenbaker's ridicule soon forced the Liberals to dissolve the truth squad. Voters who could not bring themselves to support the Conservatives turned in some cases to the NDP and Social Credit rather than to the Liberals.

Nevertheless when the votes were counted on April 8, 1963, Canada had a new Prime Minister: Lester Bowles Pearson. The Liberals had climbed to 129 seats and the Conservatives had dropped to 95. It was another minority government. With only four more seats the Liberals would have been in a majority position and would not have had to rely on the two minor parties for support. The knowledge that a more effective campaign would probably have won these four seats took some of the edge off the Liberals' celebration.

Even so it was a great day for Lester Pearson. The son of a Methodist minister, the former diplomat, the reluctant politician now found himself at the summit of Canada's political system, the country's fourteenth Prime Minister. He had come a long way since his first day as Liberal leader in 1958 when he had been almost destroyed by John Diefenbaker and from his first election campaign when he had led his party to an unprecedented disaster. Through hard work he had rebuilt the Liberal party organization. With persistence he had learned how to handle himself in the House of Commons. With courage he had faced his critics on the hustings. He still disliked the in-fighting and the emotional appeals expected of a party leader, but he had adjusted sufficiently well to the political arena that it no longer repelled or frightened him as it had in the beginning.

Pearson was inspired by the opportunities that his newly acquired position gave him to serve the interests of his country. He had encountered a succession of fortuitous circumstances in his life, of which he had taken advantage because of his inborn sense of duty. Now he had a long and ambitious list of policies to put into operation. In the international field he wished to restore the prestige Canada had lost under John Diefenbaker. (An American journalist in London remarked: 'It is scarcely an exaggeration to say that fewer tears were shed [in England] over the fall of Canadian Prime Minister Diefenbaker than over the upset of any major Commonwealth political figure since Oliver Cromwell.') At home he had an ambitious program of social reform that he wanted to introduce, and there was the pressing need to satisfy an increasingly restless Québec.

As Canadians went to bed on April 8, most were reassurred by the fact that the Liberals were in power—or at least that the Conservatives were not. Pearson had promised an exciting and productive 'sixty days of decision' and the country looked forward eagerly to a government that would get things done in a decisive way. The people had given Lester Pearson their trust and were hopeful, even confident, that he would not let them down.

5

Prime Minister: 1963~5

On April 22, 1963, fourteen days after the election that had swept John Diefenbaker out of power, Lester Pearson was sworn in as Canada's fourteenth Prime Minister. Shortly before noon the twenty-five men and one woman who were to form the new Cabinet began to arrive at Rideau Hall, the residence of the Governor General in Ottawa, to take their oath of office. Pearson, dressed in a morning coat, arrived in an appropriately official-looking Buick. The group was then led upstairs to the Governor General's bedroom, where General Vanier was recuperating from a mild heart attack. Bibles were distributed by the Clerk of the Privy Council, the oath of office was administered, and each signed the official book. The new Cabinet ministers were then led back downstairs, where they had a glass of sherry with Madame Vanier and assembled for a group picture. Afterwards, in a small drawingroom crowded with reporters and television cameras, the new Prime Minister and his Cabinet were introduced to the press.

The country seemed delighted at the prospect of a new government that would restore order and prosperity to the nation. Although the government was a minority one, it had come into office with the support of the country's journalistic, business, academic, and bureaucratic élites. Newspapers (such as the Toronto *Globe and Mail*) that had long supported the

Conservative party turned against John Diefenbaker to support the Liberals on election day. Canada's financial leaders were confident that economic stability would be restored once the Liberals were in power. Canadian academics viewed Pearson as one of their own and trusted that he would restore Canada's prestige with the rest of the world. The Ottawa bureaucracy also felt more comfortable with the new government after the mutual suspicion that had existed during the previous administration. The feeling that the Diefenbaker government had left the country with economic chaos and a weakened world image increased expectations that everything would be all right again once Pearson took over. Seldom had a new government's image been more favourable and its accomplishments more widely predicted. An Ottawa *Citizen* reporter wrote that 'Pearson and his ministers will come to power equipped with sheaves of policy papers, priority lists and agendas which they expect will enable the quickest take-off of any new Government in Canada's history.'

After the newly sworn-in members of the Pearson government had had lunch, they assembled in the historic Privy Council chamber of the East Block for their first Cabinet meeting. Pearson seated himself in the highbacked leather chair that had been used by every Prime Minister since John A. Macdonald, while the other ministers seated themselves around the oval table in order of seniority. On the Prime Minister's right were Paul Martin, the new Secretary of State for External Affairs, and Paul Hellyer, the Minister of Defence. On his left were Jack Pickersgill, who had taken the relatively light Secretary-of-State portfolio to allow him time to concentrate on the important job of being his party's leader in the House of Commons; Walter Gordon, the Minister of Finance; and George McIlraith, the Minister of

Prime Minister Pearson with his Cabinet, April 22, 1963. In the front row are Paul Hellyer, J. W. Pickersgill, Senator Ross Macdonald, Lionel

Transport. With the exception of Gordon, who had worked for the Liberals behind the scenes and had been elected to Parliament for the first time in 1963, these were the men who had been Pearson's staunch supporters in Parliament during their shared years of frustration in opposition to the Diefenbaker government. Pearson's Québec lieutenant, who was expected to advise him on how to deal with that province, was Lionel Chevrier, the Justice Minister. One of the most promising new ministers was Maurice Lamontagne, President of the Privy Council, who had been Pearson's chief economic adviser in Opposition and, as a respected economist and intellectual, personified the promise of the new government. Another interesting member of the Cabinet was Guy Favreau, a Montreal lawyer who was first given the immigration portfolio; he carried out his duties so well that in 1964 he was made Minister of Justice, House Leader, and the Prime Minister's Québec lieutenant—a staggering burden that soon proved too much for him to bear. The one woman in the Cabinet was Judy LaMarsh, an outspoken and sometimes indiscreet lawyer from Niagara Falls who was appointed Minister of National Health and Welfare.

The Cabinet met with the knowledge that the Liberal election slogan of 'Sixty Days of Decision' meant that a great deal of work had to be done in a very short time. The experienced members of the government knew that it was usually difficult to accomplish things quickly in Ottawa, partly because the large bureaucracy seemed incapable of moving quickly, but also because new policies required careful study and planning if they were to be effective. Nevertheless the public had been led to expect quick results from the new government, and Pearson instructed his ministers to swing their departments into action.

Pearson's immediate personal concern was to restore the sense of friendship in Canada's relations with the United States and Great Britain that had been eroded by John Diefenbaker. This had been one of the main promises of his election campaign, and he was passionately committed to it, believing that foreign affairs was one of the areas in which the Diefenbaker government had performed the worst. His technique for this project of diplomatic fence-mending was to visit both England and the U.S., which he did in early May. In London Pearson met with the Prime Minister, was made a Privy Councillor by the Queen and discussed trade matters, which had been one of the major causes of the previous Canadian-British disagreements. Pearson saw his trip as an opportunity to acquaint himself with current conditions and, above all, to use his long-time friendships in the British government and his diplomatic ability to restore good relations. In this task he appeared to be remarkably successful. The *Sunday Times* commented that Pearson had 'at a stroke restored the sense of intimate and understanding partnership that Britons used to associate with Canada. All trace of the quarrels and tension that unhappily characterized Mr Diefenbaker's Conservative rule seems to have been swept away by his visit.'

Five days after returning to Ottawa from London, Pearson left for a meeting with President Kennedy at his summer home at Hyannis Port, Massachusetts. Since the American president and John Diefenbaker had developed a personal distaste for one another that soured Canadian-American relations in the early 1960s, Pearson was anxious to establish a good personal relationship with Kennedy and also to settle the troublesome issue of nuclear weapons. The friendly mood of the meetings was quickly established when, while the two leaders' aides were with them, Pearson began

Pearson with President John F. Kennedy at Hyannis Port, May 10, 1963.

exchanging baseball stories and statistics with one of Kennedy's assistants, Dave Powers. As each tried to outdo the other, it became clear that Pearson had an extensive knowledge of baseball history and folklore. 'He'll do,' Kennedy remarked as the baseball discussion continued. Pearson later recalled with pleasure that while at Hyannis Port the President had taken him for a walk down a long path until they reached a flagpole where the Presidential flag flew while the U.S. leader was in residence. Kennedy removed the flag, folded it, and gave it to Pearson as a memento of the visit, a gesture that Pearson interpreted as an indication that Canadian – American relations were once again on a solid footing. During the actual discussions Pearson kept his election promise and agreed to begin negotiations with the U.S. government for the acceptance by Canada of American nuclear weapons. (These negotiations were finally completed in August 1963.) Two Canada – U.S. Cabinet Committees on defence and economic affairs were reactivated in an attempt to restore a sense of co-operation and close communication between the two countries, and questions of trade and resource development were also discussed. Following Pearson's visit the American columnist Walter Lippman wrote: 'The general effect of the meeting at Hyannis Port has been that of a good scrubbing and a cool shower after a muddy brawl.' Although he was later to be criticized at home for adopting too co-operative an attitude towards the United States at this meeting, Pearson had accomplished his immediate objectives of restoring harmony in Canada's relations with its two major allies.

Meanwhile officials in Ottawa were working feverishly on the preparation of a Throne Speech that would contain the promise of enough dynamic action to match the expectations aroused by the election slogan, 'Sixty Days of Decision'. But while the speech contained exciting promises, such as the introduction of a nation-wide pension plan, it was Finance Minister Gordon's budget, presented on June 13, that aroused the greatest interest and soon provided the government with its first of many crises. Gordon, a close friend of Pearson's and one of the main architects of the rebuilding of the Liberal party after its 1958 collapse, was suspicious of the civil servants in the Department of Finance, whom he considered overly cautious and hesitant to try new approaches. Feeling that the Department's advice did not 'reflect the spirit of the 60 days', and wishing to produce his first budget in two months instead of the usual four, he did most of his work in his House of Commons office rather than his departmental one and brought in three bright economists and accountants from the private sector to assist him.

The new Finance Minister's maiden budget was not only the financial accounting of the government but the first public indication of its planned direction of the economy. There was little opposition to the removal of the 11-per-cent federal sales-tax exemption for building materials, an attempt to help balance the accounts after the Diefenbaker government had added $3 billion to the national debt; nor was there opposition to several announced measures to stimulate the economy, such as a special allowance for employers who hired workers over forty-five years of age who had been unemployed for six months or more. These policies made little impact compared with Gordon's proposed measures to halt the growing U.S. takeover of Canadian businesses. The budget proposed a 30-per-cent takeover tax and various tax changes to decrease the growing trend towards foreign control. Gordon was convinced that foreign ownership of the Canadian economy would eventually weaken Canada's political independence by limiting the country's freedom to make its own decisions. He pointed out that almost two-thirds of the country's manufacturing capacity was owned by foreigners, mostly American, while the percentage of foreign ownership in such industries as petroleum and mining was in the high nineties.

Pearson, on the other hand, was not an economic nationalist. Believing that nationalism was anachronistic and that complete economic sovereignty would reduce Canada's standard of living by at least 25 per cent, he favoured co-operation with the United States on economic matters and did not believe that Canada's *political* independence was lessened by its *economic* dependence on the United States. However, although personally uncomfortable with the kind of nationalism represented by Gordon's measures, Pearson himself approved the budget when he saw the first draft, saying that the takeover tax would give it 'some kick' and that Canadian – American relations were sufficiently good since his visit to Hyannis Port to survive this new policy.

Neither Pearson nor Gordon foresaw the intense criticism these measures were to provoke. The attempts to restrict U.S. investment in Canada were attacked in the West and the Maritimes, where it was argued that only with American capital could these regions reach levels of prosperity that central Canada had already attained; in Québec, where the provincial government seemed more interested in lessening the dominance of Montreal's English-Canadian community than in reducing U.S. ownership of the economy; and by businessmen, who felt that their prosperity and that of Canada depended on the closest economic co-operation with the United States. But it was Walter Gordon's errors in procedure, even more than his overestimation of the degree of economic nationalism in Canada, that caused him the most trouble. As the stock market began to plunge, Gordon, fearing a full-scale financial crisis, decided to withdraw the takeover tax. But he made the mistake of announcing the withdrawal nineteen minutes before the eastern stock markets closed, which allowed some traders to make large profits as the stocks moved upward in price once again. Gordon had violated a parliamentary tradition that any major announcements that might affect trading be made only after the stock markets had closed. Opposition members of Parliament also seized on the fact that the budget had been prepared by three 'outsiders' who were not members of the public service; when they learned that two had remained in their companies' employ while working on the budget, they charged that there was a conflict of interest. The combination of Gordon's departure from established tradition and the controversial takeover tax resulted in calls for his resignation from several major newspapers and financial leaders. Even the Cabinet began to split into pro- and anti-Gordon factions. On June 20—the sixtieth day, ironically, since the new government had assumed office—Gordon went to the Prime Minister and offered to resign if Pearson felt he was too great an embarrassment to the government. Pearson replied that a transfer of portfolios might be appropriate, but Gordon refused to consider such a course and the matter rested. The controversy had seriously damaged the government's credibility and had destroyed the spirit of optimism and confidence that had swept through the country when it had first taken office. Now it was seen to be a government like any other, composed of mortal, fallible people. Pearson's own prestige suffered little during this affair, but some observers considered him weak for not having immediately demanded Gordon's resignation.

A major social trend in Canada during the 1960s was the

steady growth in urban areas. Whereas in 1939 one out of every three workers was employed in agriculture, by 1960 only one in eight earned a living on the farm. According to the 1961 census, two out of every three Canadians lived in urban areas. Small towns declined as young people moved to the cities to find jobs. The post-war flow of immigrants also contributed to the trend, since most of them settled in the large cities. Urbanization brought with it a need for greater governmental involvement in its citizens' lives. Neighbours could no longer be counted on for help as they could on the farm, and in this new environment the state was the only instrument capable of providing the social services that could assist the old, the poor, and the sick. The Canadian government's social-security system had been gradually growing, but it made a large step forward during the Pearson administration. One of its major innovations was the introduction of the Canada Pension Plan, which proposed that retirement pensions be made available to practically everyone who was working. This had been part of the Liberal election platform, but it soon became apparent that the plan could not be instituted immediately. Since social security was the responsibility of the provinces, according to the usual interpretation of the British North America Act, this kind of national program could be introduced only with the co-operation of the provinces. The government therefore issued a White Paper that was designed to explain the scheme in layman's language. The Canada Pension Plan came into force on May 5, 1965, after a difficult series of negotiations with Québec. The government also introduced plans for a $400-million municipal development and loan fund in an attempt to assist the provinces, most of which were experiencing financial problems. Here too, however, lengthy negotiations were necessary before the plan could be implemented.

The catchy slogan 'Sixty Days of Decision' had created the unrealistic illusion that the government would transform the country during its first two months in office. But such expectations did not take into account the fact that the rules of Parliament allotted specific periods of time for debates on the Speech from the Throne and for the granting of supply, which could not be put aside; that legislation could not be enacted immediately because of the need for careful planning or the securing of provincial agreement; and that much of the government's time in the House of Commons was taken up by non-legislative matters such as the establishment of a Parliamentary Defence Committee, which Pearson had promised during the election campaign. By the end of the government's first sixty days, only four important bills had been passed and public disillusionment could be detected. The press contributed to the damage caused by the unwise slogan by keeping a regular 'box-score' of the government's day-by-day accomplishments; it even went so far as to ask Pearson if Sundays counted in the sixty-day period.

The growth of nationalist and separatist sentiment in Québec provided the Pearson government with its greatest challenge, and was the area in which Pearson's diplomatic talents were most needed and most successful. English-speaking Canada first became aware that something was happening in Québec when terrorists planted bombs in some public buildings and mailboxes in Montreal. The most dramatic indication that conditions had changed, however, came when the Queen visited Québec City in 1964 and was met by a large hostile crowd. The anger of the demonstrators and the apathy shown by ordinary Québec citizens towards the Queen shocked many English Canadians. Extreme statements from both sides caused a further deterioration in English-French relations. A Montreal French-language newspaper stated: 'The time has come for the verbal revolution in Québec to pass from words to action,' which prompted an English-Canadian Senator to retort: 'Okay, if that's the way they want it, we'll keep a 10-mile corridor on both sides of the St Lawrence and let them wither on the vine.' As bombs continued to explode in Montreal, English Canada wondered if a full-scale revolution was in the making in Québec.

The outbreak of terrorism was only a small reflection of the large-scale changes that were taking place in the province. Fundamentally Québec was experiencing the trials and tribulations of its entry into the twentieth century. The Union Nationale government, which had gained power in the province in 1936, had encouraged the maintenance of Québec's traditions—its reliance on agriculture and the dominant position of the Catholic Church—as a means of retaining power. Following the death of Premier Duplessis in 1959, a Liberal government under Jean Lesage was elected in 1960. Lesage was determined to use the powers of the state to improve conditions within the province. He set out to remove education from the control of the Church, to increase the size of the civil service so that it could carry out needed social reforms, and to nationalize some public utilities. All of this, however, required money, and herein lay the source of the conflict between Ottawa and Québec City that was to dominate the first years of the Pearson administration. By 1963 the expenditures of the Québec government had risen to $954 million, compared to $553 million in 1959, and exceeded available revenues by some $91 million. Despite efforts to raise money through increased taxes and borrowing, Québec's financial resources were still inadequate for the large public expenditures that Lesage felt were necessary to modernize the province. His government concluded that the only source of additional money was the federal government.

This situation coincided with similar financial problems in almost all the other provinces. At the time of Confederation the federal government had been given most of the expensive responsibilities and taxing powers. As the years passed, however, those areas in which the provinces had jurisdiction—social security, highway construction, and education—assumed an importance that had not been foreseen in 1867. The cost of providing these services greatly strained provincial treasuries. Although Québec's requirements were most apparent because of its energetic new policies, all provinces were facing the need for additional sources of revenue. It was the misfortune of the Pearson government to be in power at a time when the provinces were making the strongest demands on Ottawa since the early days of the Second World War.

The demands of Québec, while inspired by some problems that were similar to those of the other provinces, had to be dealt with in a very special way. The sense of accomplishment that Jean Lesage's 'quiet revolution' of modernization instilled in Quebeckers had troublesome side-effects. Some Quebeckers began to argue that now that the province had shown itself capable of making needed reforms, it was time for it to become independent of the rest of Canada, for only then could the survival of the French language in Québec be guaranteed. Although only a very small percentage of Quebeckers favoured separatism, there were many more who felt that English Canada had to prove that it could accommodate the aspirations of the 'awakened' Québec, which was no longer willing to have its economy controlled by English Canadians and many of its political decisions made by a federal government in which English Canadians were dominant. This, and not the scattered terrorist bombings, was the real crisis faced by the Canadian Confederation during the first half of the 1960s. It remained to be seen whether the Pearson government could respond to this challenge. If it could not provide sufficiently imaginative policies, the separation of Québec from the rest of Canada would likely result.

The policy that Pearson soon developed was known as 'co-operative federalism'. Many of its details were provided by Pearson's French-Canadian advisers—notably Maurice Lamontagne, Lionel Chevrier, and Guy Favreau—but the spirit of compromise on which it was based was very much a reflection of Pearson's own style. In the Throne Speech debate of February 1964 Pearson stressed that only through constant co-operation and consultation could this problem be resolved. This policy meant in practice that in every area under provincial jurisdiction in which the federal government wished to become involved, it would take care to consult the provinces beforehand, collaborate with them in the drafting of any legislation, and co-ordinate implementation with them. Nothing would be forced upon them. If a province did not wish to participate in a federal program, it would be allowed to 'opt out' and to institute its own program with money obtained from the federal government. This approach would be extremely time-consuming and frustrating for federal officials who wanted things to be done quickly, but Pearson argued that patience was necessary. The result was that, in many cases, Québec received from Ottawa the money it wanted to undertake various social programs; but it did not receive anything to which it was not entitled under the British North America Act, for all so-called special arrangements made with Québec were also available to the other nine provinces if they so wished. This co-operative arrangement, which satisfied no one fully and was often criticized by both English and French Canadians, helped to assure French Canadians that the federal government was sympathetic to their concerns, while it gained time for English Canadians to become accustomed to the idea that French Canada would henceforth be playing a much more active role in the affairs of the country.

During its first eighteen months in office the Pearson government held 114 federal-provincial consultations at all levels—more than had been called during the entire six years of the Diefenbaker administration. Meetings of first ministers became a regular part of the Ottawa scene. The standard procedure was for the Prime Minister to offer a formal dinner for the premiers at his residence on the first night, followed by a dinner given by the Governor General the next night, and a cocktail party for all the participants on the final evening. The meetings themselves were usually held in the ornate Confederation Room of the West Block of the Parliament Buildings, where crystal chandeliers and rich red draperies added a touch of pomp. As conference chairman, Pearson was unexcelled. His long diplomatic experience, his ability to lighten tense situations with a disarming quip, and his sense of the right moment to push forward with a position or to yield gracefully kept many a conference from breaking up in chaos and disharmony. The very fact that issues such as tax-sharing arrangements, social-security reform, and procedures for amending the constitution were being negotiated around a bargaining table strengthened Pearson's hand, for he was able to employ the same techniques of conciliation that he had used so effectively as a diplomat. The journalist Peter Newman commented: 'By treating relations between Québec and the rest of Canada as an exercise in foreign affairs involving the clash of nationalistic forces, he was able to make

the large adjustments involved and to sponsor his own version
of a political cease-fire. None of the tough problems of disunity
were actually resolved. But just as in his Suez solution he temporarily prevented a shooting war, Pearson gained the vital
time for a more enduring settlement of Canada's internal problems.'

Of all the critical issues that were resolved through the
spirit of co-operative federalism, none was more important
than the pension-plan dispute of 1964. The year before, the
Pearson government had introduced its proposed Canada
Pension Plan, only to encounter particularly strong opposition from Québec, which wished to use the accumulated
funds for public investment in the province. After a series of
meetings failed to resolve the main problem, a federal-
provincial conference was called for Québec City on March
31, 1964. It appeared that, if the federal government imposed
its policy, the Lesage government would be placed in a
position where a break with Ottawa would be almost inevitable; on the other hand an agreement that gave in completely
to Québec's wishes would have shown the inability of the
federal government to legislate necessary social policies for
the entire country. When the Québec City conference ended,
no agreement had been reached. Lesage had made a particularly blunt demand for a larger share of tax revenues, and the
task force that had prepared the province's own pension-plan
proposals had done its work so thoroughly that federal officials were unable to demonstrate that the federal plan was
any better. When he reported back to the House of Commons, Pearson was severely criticized by members of the
opposition parties for his failure to achieve agreement in
Québec City. When John Diefenbaker asked if the government intended to proceed with the pension plan in spite of

the 'fiasco' at Québec City, the Prime Minister could do little more than retort with a quip. 'I will ignore the right honourable gentleman's introduction to this question about the conference,' he said, 'except to say that I recognize his authority to speak on conference fiascos.' The 'crisis of Confederation' had reached a peak. It remained to be seen whether anything could be done to stop the trend towards disintegration that was developing in the country.

Well aware of the gravity of the situation, Pearson attempted to begin the healing process with a major speech on April 14 during the budget debate. He attempted to convince both English and French Canadians that only through compromise could conflicting goals be harmonized and the unity of the country preserved. He began by reminding the House that, in a federal system, the central government must be strong enough to discharge its responsibilities while at the same time taking care not to encroach on the jurisdiction of the provinces. If the federal government were to oppose the right of a province to withdraw from any joint program involving a matter under provincial jurisdiction, such action would not strengthen Confederation and could destroy it. He then went on to stress, as no other Prime Minister had ever done, the special position and needs of Québec. That province, he said, is 'in a very real sense the guardian of its cultural and religious and linguistic rights.' Failure to appreciate the 'special sensitiveness' of Québec would 'soon and finally destroy Confederation and make impossible the growth, in strength and unity, of a Canadian nation.' Finally, Pearson said, there must also be 'great concessions and compromises' on the part of both the provincial governments and the government in Ottawa. 'It is the task of Parliament, without regard to party; it is the challenge of statesmanship rising above faction, to find

the solutions to our problems, which are now more serious and
more difficult than any we have faced in peace time since
1867.'

Pearson's impassioned plea for tolerance and the sincerity
with which he spoke had a dramatic effect. Douglas Fisher,
an NDP member and one of the government's fiercest critics,
said afterwards that he had intended to start his own speech
by 'scorching the Prime Minister', but that Pearson's speech,
'which was quite candid, certainly constructive and somewhat
conciliatory', had made him feel that the Prime Minister
'does know the dangers and does feel they are matters which
time and negotiation will solve, and that he and all of us
have a concept of Canadianism which enables us to join with
him in fighting for it.' French-Canadian MPs and editorialists were equally impressed. A writer for Montreal's *La
Presse* said that Pearson was risking his popularity with the
rest of Canada in order 'to make of Confederation a régime
that is more in harmony with the aspirations of Québec and
French Canada in general.'

Pearson's attempt to improve the atmosphere was matched
by a last-ditch effort to produce an acceptable pension-plan
compromise. It seemed hopeless, for Lesage was preparing to
deliver a violent attack on Ottawa in a budget speech that was
scheduled to be given only a few days later. Nevertheless the
Prime Minister agreed to let his top adviser, Tom Kent, and
Forestry Minister Sauvé, a good friend of several Québec officials, fly to Québec City in a final attempt to settle the crisis.
Lesage, impressed by Ottawa's willingness to compromise on
some important matters, immediately agreed to postpone the
date of his budget presentation and sent his negotiators to
Ottawa to work out a final settlement. On April 20 Pearson
announced that the two governments had come to an accord.

Ottawa had agreed to make more tax revenues, plus control over the pension-plan reserve fund, available to the provinces, while Québec in turn had agreed to certain modifications in its own pension plan to make it more similar to the federal one. The agreement was hailed as a major accomplishment by all parties in the House of Commons. New Democratic Party leader T. C. Douglas called it 'a real victory for national unity', and even John Diefenbaker admitted that it was 'a step forward'. Jean Lesage expressed pride that Québec had finally been recognized as a province 'with a special status in Confederation'. The influential editor of the Montreal newspaper *Le Devoir*, Claude Ryan, wrote: 'Are we at a turning point in the history of Confederation? It is too early to be able to make such a big statement. But at least a ray of light has appeared. Let us rejoice.'

Tensions between Ottawa and Québec City, which had almost reached the breaking point in April 1964, gradually subsided after the pension-plan agreement. By 1968 Québec received 50 per cent of personal income taxes collected in that province by the federal government compared to 17 per cent in 1963; 10 per cent of the corporation taxes compared to 9 per cent; and 75 percent of the succession duties compared to 50 per cent. The various opting-out agreements that were negotiated appeared to satisfy the Québec government's desire that it should have enough money to implement policies that would reflect the province's particular needs, although differences of opinion continued to emerge that required careful handling. Pearson's conciliatory approach was largely responsible for defusing discontent within the province. Lesage seemed convinced that Québec could obtain its goals by co-operating with Ottawa. Those who disagreed with him, such as Resources Minister René Lévesque, were obliged to leave the provincial Liberals and form their own sep-aratist party.

Once the crisis posed by Québec had diminished, Pearson was left with the task of convincing English Canadians— most of whom had very little appreciation of the changes that were occurring within Québec—that he had not compro-mised too much. The Royal Commission on Bilingualism and Biculturalism, which the Pearson government had estab-lished in 1963 to recommend ways in which Confederation could be developed on the basis of 'an equal partnership between the two founding races', was attacked by many English Canadians as a waste of time and money. Unaware of the very limited extent to which French Canadians were represented in the power structure in Ottawa, many failed to recognize that there was some justification in French Canadi-ans' complaints that they did not have the power they should have. A more valid criticism of the 'B and B Commission' was that its original terms of reference failed to take account of the large number of Canadians whose origins were neither English nor French. Pearson later realized that this oversight might be interpreted as an attempt to relegate them to sec-ond-class status. In a number of speeches he emphasized that Canada possessed two 'historic *language* groups' but that people of all ethnic origins could preserve their own *cultural* traits within either. This was a difficult concept for many to grasp. In western Canada particularly, where many people of neither English nor French origin had settled, the B and B Commission was considered to be an example of the federal government's 'weak' attitude towards Québec. Inevitably traces of bigotry and extremism became visible. One of Pearson's bit-terest critics was a Member of Parliament from his own party, Ralph Cowan. Asked by a reporter one day why things seemed rather quiet in the Parliament Buildings, Cowan exploded: 'I'll tell you why it's quiet. It's quiet because Pearson's giving the Frenchmen every blankety-blank thing they want. They go home at night and dream it up. They ask for it in the morning and, in the afternoon, Pearson gives it to them.' Although disappointed by his inability to convince all English Canadians to accept his co-operative policies towards Québec, Pearson believed they were necessary if Confederation was to be maintained, and he did not cease his efforts to promote this view across the country.

The resolution of the pension-plan dispute with Québec gave the Pearson government a much-needed boost in prestige, and its supporters hoped it would now be able to demonstrate the initiative that the Liberals had promised in the 1963 election campaign. Realizing that his government was acquiring the reputation of being capable of little more than responding to crises, Pearson resolved to be more decisive in the future.

One of his decisions was to support Paul Hellyer's imaginative concept to unify the three branches of the Canadian Armed Forces—army, navy, and air force—under one command. The new Minister of National Defence believed that such a step would prevent unnecessary duplication of activities and save the country money. Legislation was passed in July 1964 for the creation of an integrated defence structure, but it was not until 1966 that the Opposition realized this was only a first step towards the eventual disappearance of the identitites of the three forces. When Hellyer repeated his intention to establish 'one force with one common name, a common uniform and common rank designations', senior army, naval, and air force officers delivered stinging public attacks on the plan, which, they said, would destroy the morale of the armed forces.

The issue received extensive publicity for several months, but Hellyer refused to yield. Peter Newman concluded that 'It will take a decade to evaluate the real worth of Hellyer's unification program, but viewed strictly as one of the more daring attacks on the status quo, the plan should be judged as one of the really imaginative experiments of the Pearson ministry.'

While Pearson's greatest knowledge and experience lay in the field of foreign affairs, he had little personal involvement in the conduct of Canada's external activities during his period as Prime Minister. Most of his time was necessarily spent dealing with the various internal crises and issues that confronted his government; he was obliged to leave foreign policy largely in the hands of his Secretary of State for External Affairs, Paul Martin. But Canada itself was less active on the international scene than it had been in the early 1950s, when Pearson had won fame as foreign minister. After the Second World War, Canada had emerged as one of the most powerful countries in the world; its economy had been strengthened, not ravaged, by the war, and it was ideally suited to participate in the many peace-keeping activites of the newly created United Nations Organization. By the early 1960s, Western Europe had regained its economic strength, Japan and China had emerged as potential world powers, and a multitude of newly independent states in Africa and Asia were determined to gain world attention. Above all, the days of optimism that the United Nations could guarantee world peace had faded into despair. The UN's role as a peacekeeper was diminished by the growing number of civil conflicts in which it was powerless to intervene, and by procedural and financial problems. Opportunities for Canada to act as an international peacekeeper were therefore few and far between.

The one exception to the general inactivity of the United Nations in this field came in 1964. Following the outbreak of fighting on the Mediterranean island of Cyprus between Greeks and Cypriots, the UN authorized the sending of a supervisory force to keep the two sides apart. The same day President Lyndon Johnson phoned Pearson to stress the need for Canadian participation in the operation. Only Canada, he told the Prime Minister, could provide enough troops and get them there quickly enough. Pearson, convinced that this was precisely the kind of peace-keeping activity in which the United Nations should become involved, went to the House of Commons when the evening sitting began on March 13. He had already instructed the military to begin preparations for an air-lift of troops to Cyprus but he needed the consent of Parliament. The Prime Minister arrived just as the sitting began at 8 p.m., before many of the MPs had yet returned from supper, so that there would be less chance of anyone's opposing his proposal. The handful of members who were in the House gave the required unanimous consent and the military preparations, which had already begun, were continued. Later that night President Johnson, greatly impressed by the speed with which Canada had acted, phoned Pearson again. 'Now,' the U.S. President enquired, 'what can I do for you?' The prompt arrival of the United Nations Force in Cyprus succeeded in preventing the fighting from reaching crisis proportions and Canadian forces were still in Cyprus ten years later. It was a clear example of the United Nation's potential for preventing war, but the only time during Pearson's years in power when it was able to take such action. This was also one of the few occasions when Pearson was involved directly in foreign-policy matters as Prime Minister. As the excitement of the successful Cyprus operation died down, his attention and that of the country returned to domestic matters.

In the spring of 1964 the government's legislative program

was badly bogged down in Parliament with no less than thirty untouched bills on the order paper. Despite the momentary success of the Cyprus operation, the government was still reeling from its budgetary and legislative reverses. It was at this point that Pearson decided to take a personal initiative. The Liberal party's 1962 and 1963 election platforms had promised that legislation for a distinctive Canadian flag would be introduced within two years of the party's taking office. Pearson therefore announced in May 1964— without consulting Cabinet—his intention of submitting to Parliament a maple-leaf design to replace the Red Ensign as Canada's flag. Few announcements could have aroused a more emotional response. Millions of Canadians—or so it seemed from the tide of criticism that greeted his announcement—favoured retaining the Red Ensign, with the Union Jack of Great Britain in the top left-hand corner. For some Canadians the Red Ensign represented their ties with their country of origin; for others it was the flag under which they had fought during the last world war. Still others opposed a new flag because they believed it represented an attempt by the government to 'appease Québec', which was understandably reluctant to express pride in a flag that resembled that of Great Britain. The 'flag debate' dominated the news for a full half year in Canada and preoccupied Parliament for almost as long. It was an emotional issue that, once again, brought into question the solidarity of the Canadian Confederation.

With a great deal of courage, Pearson chose to make the initial announcement of his plan to the Royal Canadian Legion in Winnipeg. The Prime Minister knew that the Legion, composed of veterans of previous wars in which Canada had participated, would be particularly hostile, but he thought that his main critics had the right to hear his statement first. He realized too that the encounter would provide great publicity for his proposal. Speaking with passion and conviction, Pearson told the meeting that he believed 'most sincerely that it is time now for Canadians to unfurl a flag that is truly distinctive and truly national in character; as Canadian as the maple leaf which should be its dominant design; a flag easily identifiable as Canada's; a flag which cannot be mistaken for the emblem of any other country....' The Union Jack, he said, should continue to be flown in Canada, not as a national flag but as a symbol of Canada's membership in the Commonwealth and of its loyalty to the Crown. Despite his argument that the acceptance of a new flag did not imply any disrespect for the Union Jack or for Canada's history, Pearson was almost drowned out by boos and insults from the audience. But he went on with his speech. This confrontation won him a great deal of sympathy and admiration throughout the country. Even some of those who disagreed with his policy were forced to admire his courage and conviction. 'In the last week,' wrote columnist Charles Lynch, 'Mr Pearson has been enjoying himself as only a man can who has fixed a course that he is certain is right, that suits his own personal feelings, and that he is convinced will be for the good of the country.'

Having committed the government to the concept of a flag with a maple leaf, Pearson next proposed a specific design, for he knew that if he left this to a parliamentary committee the matter might never be settled. His suggestion (originally made to him by a Liberal Member of Parliament) was for a flag consisting of three red maple leaves on a white background, with a blue stripe on both sides representing the Atlantic and Pacific oceans. On June 12 the new design was test flown with mixed reactions. A public-opinion poll showed that 56 per cent of Canadians who were questioned favoured retaining the Red Ensign, while only 44 per cent favoured a distinctive Canadian flag.

The flag debate occupied Parliament during most of the summer and fall of 1964. Pearson began it in June by appealing for the adoption of a distinctive flag that would symbolize 'a Canada united, strong, independent and equal to her task'. Opposition leader Diefenbaker moved an amendment to Pearson's motion, calling for the matter to be submitted to a national plebiscite. After a short break to deal with other matters, the House continued the debate on August 12. Members of the New Democratic Party criticized the government for spending so much time on the subject of the flag; they believed important social legislation should be given priority, although many of them supported the proposed design. Much of their criticism was reserved for the Conservatives, whom they accused of obstructing the work of Parliament. Although the rules of the Commons stipulated that no member could speak more than once on a given motion, each amendment or sub-amendment to the original motion allowed him to speak again, and the Conservatives made great use of this provision. Members spoke several times, repeating the same arguments and preventing the proposal from coming to a vote, for the Conservatives hoped that the government would give in to mounting public opposition and withdraw the measure. They also saw it as a possible way of defeating the government, and as an issue on which to fight the next election. When the debate finally ended in December every Conservative MP except two had spoken at least once, three had spoken five times, seven had spoken four times, and nineteen had spoken three times. In all, 92 Conservatives made 195 speeches during the debate, 34 Liberals spoke 41 times, 10 NDP members made 17 speeches, 8 Social Credit MPs delivered 12, and 6 Créditiste members spoke 13 times. It was an exhausting and time-consuming process, during which the other work of Parliament all but ground to a halt.

Pearson attempted to end the marathon debate in August by announcing that a free vote would be held on the flag issue. This meant that no member of the Liberal party would be bound by party discipline to support the government's policy, and that a defeat on this issue would not be interpreted by the government as cause to resign. The NDP leader described the proposal as a 'major concession', but the Conservatives said that the offer had come too late. However, Diefenbaker later agreed with T. C. Douglas's proposal that the matter should be referred for study to a committee composed of members of all parties.

The 'flag committee' held forty-five meetings in less than six weeks. By mid-October, after reviewing more than two thousand designs that had been submitted to it, the Committee had narrowed its choice to three: the three maple leaves with a blue border (now referred to as the 'Pearson pennant'), the Red Ensign, and a new design featuring a single red maple leaf on a white background with red borders. This last design had been proposed by a history professor from the Royal Military College in Kingston and was an adaptation of the college's banner. When the three designs were put to a vote in the Committee, the Red Ensign was defeated, supported only by the four English-speaking Conservative members present. The single maple-leaf design was then voted upon. The Conservatives, assuming that the Liberals were committed to the 'Pearson pennant', decided to vote for the new design; they hoped to embarrass the government and to show that they were not being obstructionist, although they were sure that the design would not be approved. To their shock the Liberal, NDP, Social Credit, and Créditiste members all voted for the single maple-leaf design as well and the vote was therefore unanimous. The Committee then recommended that the Union Jack be retained as a secondary flag symbolizing Canada's membership in the Commonwealth.

John Diefenbaker was unwilling to accept the flag committee's recommendations. The Conservatives continued to prevent the matter from coming to a vote in the House of Commons and the speeches continued. Although some of them enabled MPs to make stirring statements of their nationalism and provided an interesting study of the elements of Canadianism, many members were unhappy with what seemed to them to be a waste of Parliament's time. Créditiste leader Réal Caouette complained on December 1 that 'If the Canadian symbol, now represented by the maple leaf on the flag proposed by the committee which considered this question, is not satisfactory, then let us remove the maple leaf and put a beaver or a sheaf of wheat, or indeed anything else, as long as it is Canadian.' Another member, a classical scholar, lapsed into Greek at one point, leaving the interpreters speechless.

By early December Pearson decided that closure had become inevitable if Parliament was to turn its attention to other matters. He knew that governments were usually severely criticized when they cut off debate in the House, but he was convinced that the public was as tired of the matter as were most Members of Parliament. His strategy was assisted by a split that was developing in the Conservative party: Diefenbaker's Québec lieutenant, Léon Balcer, supported the introduction of closure. On the morning of December 15, the proposal for a maple-leaf flag finally came to a vote and was

Flag-raising ceremony on Parliament Hill, Ottawa, February 15, 1965. Prime Minister Pearson and Governor General Vanier are on the platform to the left.

passed 163 to 78. The battle had been a long one, but Canada finally had its own distinctive national flag.

On February 15, 1965, the Red Ensign was lowered from a flag-pole in front of the Parliament Buildings and replaced by the new maple-leaf flag as a twenty-one gun salute boomed in the distance. In a short but dramatic speech, Pearson expressed the hope that all Canadians would fly Canada's national flag with pride. He said that this day would always be remembered as 'a milestone in Canada's national progress' and that, 'As the symbol of a new chapter in our national story, our Maple Leaf Flag will also become a symbol of that unity in our country without which we cannot grow in strength and purpose.'

When Pearson looked back on his accomplishments after retiring from public life, he frequently said that the introduction of a distinctive Canadian flag was the act that had given him the most pride and satisfaction. Indeed, the new flag became the symbol of the growing pride that Canadians were feeling for their country, which culminated in a patriotic outburst during the country's centennial year.

The bitterness of the flag debate quickly passed away and the new flag was accepted by many who had opposed it in 1964. In 1966 the Canadian Legion passed a resolution supporting it, and the flag, by then a symbol of Canadian nationalism, decorated the platforms of candidates of all parties during the 1968 election. In 1967 the distinguished Canadian historian, A.R.M. Lower, wrote: 'Since the adoption of the new flag, something very interesting has happened to the Canadian psyche, something that probably cannot yet be put into words, but of whose reality sensitive minds are aware. . . . The point is simply that the country is growing up, coming to see itself as an entity, taking the interest in itself that any organism, to be healthy, must. Each time, that is, that the average citizen looks at the new flag, he unconsciously says to himself, 'That's me!'

As 1965 began, Pearson was anxious to proceed with his many proposals for social legislation that Parliament had not had time to examine. But his hopes were disappointed, for during much of the year a series of scandals, both real and alleged, dominated public attention and forced the government to spend much of its time fighting for its reputation and survival.

The main crisis revolved around a Montreal underworld figure named Lucien Rivard, who had been arrested on charges of smuggling narcotics. The Royal Canadian Mounted Police soon became suspicious that two men closely connected with the government—Raymond Denis, the executive assistant to the Minister of Immigration, and Guy Rouleau, a Member of Parliament who was acting as the Prime Minister's parliamentary secretary—had offered a bribe to one of the lawyers involved in the case to encourage him to withdraw his opposition to Rivard's release on bail. The RCMP informed the Minister of Justice, Guy Favreau, who urged them to continue their investigation. On September 2, 1964, Pearson and Favreau were returning to Ottawa on a government plane from a federal-provincial conference in Prince Edward Island. During the flight Favreau told Pearson that there were allegations of bribery involving the executive assistant to the Minister of Immigration but he did not mention any names or the fact that the issue also involved a convicted narcotics smuggler. Sixteen days later Favreau received the RCMP report on the case. After only a quick examination, he concluded that there were no grounds for laying criminal charges, even though the report strongly implicated Guy Rouleau. He told Pearson nothing more and believed the case to be closed.

However, a Progressive Conservative MP, Erik Nielsen, was told of the matter by a frustrated RCMP officer who felt it was being ignored by the government. On November 23, 1964, Nielsen raised the issue in the House of Commons. His charges caught the Liberals by surprise. Shocked at what he read in the full RCMP report on the case, the Prime Minister immediately fired Rouleau as his parliamentary secretary. The next day he was asked in the Commons when he had first been informed of the affair. Pearson replied that it had been the day before Nielsen's revelations, when Favreau had mentioned the matter to him in general terms. Pearson then left for western Canada and a previously arranged political tour.

A few days later Justice Minister Favreau revealed to his Cabinet colleagues that he had in fact mentioned the matter to Pearson during a plane flight two months earlier. Pearson was now in the position of having given false information to Parliament. Realizing that he would have to alter his answer, Pearson delayed for two weeks and then wrote a letter to the Chief Justice who was inquiring into the matter. Pearson said he had 'completely forgotten' the earlier conversation. This was plausible, for Favreau had spoken of the matter in very general terms on the plane and had not mentioned any names to indicate the seriousness of the issue; in addition, the Prime Minister was preoccupied with many other matters at the time. The Opposition capitalized on Pearson's lapse of memory, however, and strongly implied that he had knowingly lied to the House. At a news conference John Diefenbaker said: 'What would have shocked anyone else did not apparently register with the Prime Minister; for what he heard in the air, he forgot on the ground. And he continued to forget.' The Opposition moved that the whole matter be sent to the Commons Committee on Privileges and Elections to determine, in effect, whether the Prime Minister had lied to the House. Pearson was in an extremely embarrassing position, and the ruling of the Speaker against the motion was upheld by the narrow vote of 122 to 105.

Newspaper criticism of the Prime Minister was widespread. The Winnipeg *Tribune* said that he had been 'either incredibly naive and forgetful, or he was party to misleading the House of Commons.' The Toronto *Star*, generally sympathetic to the Liberals, offered this comment: 'No one who knows Mr Pearson and his career will believe that he deliberately lied to the House of Commons on November 24. Everyone who knows him will likewise accept his word that the September 2 warning slipped his mind when he made the statement. But even when his word on this matter is accepted, the fact remains that Mr Pearson has been guilty of a grave breach of his duty to Parliament in waiting for three weeks before correcting the erroneous information he had given the House. . . . There is no doubt that this business, coming on top of earlier revelations, has damaged the government heavily.'

Chief Justice Dorion's report was made public on June 29, 1965. He concluded that Raymond Denis had in fact offered a bribe to obstruct the course of justice and that Guy Rouleau had acted in a 'reprehensible' manner. The report was also critical of Justice Minister Favreau for ignoring the case when it was presented to him by the RCMP and for not submitting it to the legal advisers within his department. Favreau, whose health was deteriorating under a crushingly heavy work-load and the pressure of the inquiry, offered his resignation to the Prime Minister. Pearson originally believed that Favreau, who had been guilty of poor judgement but no wrongdoing, should remain in his portfolio. Favreau was insistent, however, and Pearson agreed. It was decided that Favreau would remain in the government but in another portfolio.

Pearson was criticized by some for not ousting Favreau from the Cabinet, since he had embarrassed the government, and by others who said that Pearson had destroyed Favreau's career by allowing him to resign from the Justice portfolio. Pearson's decision revealed a great deal about his character. He always looked at the good in people and greatly admired Favreau. He had been wary of unsupported innuendo ever since the suicide in 1957 of a close friend and fellow diplomat, Herbert Norman, who had been wrongly accused by U.S. Senator Joseph McCarthy of being a Communist. Pearson was not, by his own admission, a good disciplinarian. His daughter has recalled that, when his children got into mischief, 'he was likely to melt away or disappear behind his newspaper.' Still, he did not hesitate to fire his parliamentary secretary, Guy Rouleau, when he learned of his wrongdoing. Favreau himself did not believe, as did critics of Pearson's action such as Walter Gordon and Judy LaMarsh, that he had been let down by the Prime Minister. His letter of resignation to Pearson expressed his gratitude for Pearson's expression of confidence in suggesting that he remain in the government, and for his 'kindness and consideration and . . . unfailing support.'

No sooner had Chief Justice Dorion completed his report than the government was faced with more problems. The most embarrassing incident was the escape from prison of the very man who had provoked the scandal, Lucien Rivard. On a warm March evening, with the temperature near 40 degrees above zero, Rivard received permission from a prison guard to water the jail's skating rink. He and another prisoner quickly used the hose to slide down the prison walls and disappeared.

The federal government was in no way involved, for the jail from which Rivard escaped was under provincial jurisdiction, but the outrageous nature of his escape delighted the Opposition. Over and over again, John Diefenbaker told the story of how Rivard had been sent out to water the rink on an evening so warm the water could not freeze.

A succession of minor scandals involving government figures added further to the government's embarrassment. A junior Cabinet minister, Yvon Dupuis, was fired by Pearson for allegedly having accepted a bribe to facilitate the obtaining of a licence for a new racetrack in his constituency. Two other ministers, René Tremblay and Maurice Lamontagne, were revealed to have purchased furniture in Montreal on very easy repayment terms from a company involved in a bankruptcy scandal. The businessmen concerned had received no favours in return, but the Opposition insinuated that some 'deal' must have been involved. Since buying furniture was something the public could readily understand, it was not difficult for the Opposition to use the issue to make the government seem corrupt and inefficient. The fact that all the ministers involved in the various scandals were French Canadians injected racial overtones into the whole matter, and made it easier for disgruntled English Canadians to believe that the government was dominated by Québec.

In the midst of these scandals, Secretary of State Jack Pickersgill suggested to Pearson that he circulate to all Cabinet ministers a 'code of ethics' indicating the kind of conduct that a minister should avoid. The Prime Minister agreed. 'There is an obligation,' the report stated, 'not simply to observe the law but to act in a manner so scrupulous that it will bear the closest public scrutiny.' The document was later leaked to the press and used by the Opposition to imply that the Cabinet needed to be lectured on the proper way to behave. Nevertheless the 'code of ethics' was a useful reminder to both politicians and the public that the standards of conduct expected of a Cabinet minister were necessarily higher than those of an ordinary citizen.

It was during this time that the famous Pearson-Diefenbaker rivalry reached its peak. Although the two had often jousted verbally while Diefenbaker was Prime Minister, it was his actions as Leader of the Opposition that most antagonized Pearson. While Pearson believed that the role of an Opposition leader was to offer constructive suggestions and prove himself to be a credible alternative leader, Diefenbaker clearly thought his main role was to oppose. 'The duty of the Opposition,' he told a luncheon gathering, 'is to turn out the government.' Accordingly he sought to embarrass the government at every turn and by any means. At times his criticism was justified, but often his innuendoes ridiculed innocent men and distracted attention from more important issues. Nevertheless there was no denying that Diefenbaker was an effective Leader of the Opposition. The government was constantly harrassed by the fear of what Diefenbaker would say, for he was a master of the art of cutting invective. Pearson, despite his good nature, soon developed a passionate dislike and animosity for the man. He believed that Diefenbaker was maliciously destroying reputations and hampering the efforts of the government. At cocktail parties the Prime Minister was heard to say that he could not sleep at nights because of Diefenbaker. Pearson had never enjoyed the cut-and-thrust kind of politics in which Diefenbaker revelled and found it difficult to cope with the constant attacks levelled against his government. (His frustration was so great that, when Pearson heard rumours that Diefenbaker had once caught a 4½-pound trout at the prime ministerial residence at Harrington Lake, he tracked down a nearby resident and was delighted to learn that, although Diefenbaker had hooked the fish, he had not succeeded in landing it.) This ongoing confrontation removed from politics the little enjoyment it had ever held for Pearson. He could not comprehend the reasons for Diefenbaker's animosity towards him. Peter Newman suggested that it stemmed from the fact that Diefenbaker could never understand how a man with Pearson's obvious political liabilities could defeat him.

It was becoming clear that the various scandals and embarrassments that had plagued the government were undermining its authority. However, while John Diefenbaker was skilful at attacking the government, his ability to present his party as a credible alternative government was much poorer than Pearson's had been as Leader of the Opposition. Laurier LaPierre wrote that one of the dominant characteristics of Canadian political life in the 1960s was the apparent bankruptcy of federal leadership. Writing in the Toronto *Star*, Peter Newman said: 'The Conservatives under John Diefenbaker have lost the confidence of a majority of the Canadian people, while the Liberals under Lester Pearson have failed to gain it.' The Montreal *Gazette* expressed a common view when it said that 'Canada is fortunate in having at this time a prime minister whose good intentions are never in doubt' but that 'it might be wished that his course in the months ahead could be less "accident-prone" than it has been in the past.' A public-opinion poll in the fall of 1965 showed that three out of ten Canadians were disappointed with Pearson. Their main criticism was that he was indecisive and lacked leadership strength.

Nevertheless Pearson's minority government managed to survive in the House of Commons. The Prime Minister appealed to the NDP, the Social Credit, and the Créditistes with a diplomat's skill, complimenting some, bantering lightly with others, and replying to all with courtesy and respect. This strategy was aided immeasurably by John Diefenbaker's tendency to treat these same parties with ridicule and scorn, an approach that was hardly conducive to winning their support to overthrow the government. Furthermore a split was developing within the Conservative party itself: some members began to feel that Diefenbaker's style of confrontation was damaging both the party and the country. Although the threat of defeat was always present, Pearson was able to survive crisis after crisis and still come back for more.

By the fall of 1965 some Liberal party strategists believed that the government should call an election in order to obtain a parliamentary majority and put an end to the constant threat of defeat in the House. At least seventeen Cabinet ministers were in favour. Finance Minister Gordon was the chief advocate of an election. He argued that his latest budget, which had reduced personal income taxes by 10 per cent, had improved the government's standing in the country. Mitchell Sharp, Minister of Trade and Commerce, believed that only a stable majority government could deal with the economic problems—especially inflation—that were anticipated. In mid-August the Soviet Union signed an unexpectedly large agreement for the purchase of Canadian wheat, adding to the Liberals' hopes for gains in the West. Pearson undertook a nine-day tour of the West to test the election atmosphere. At the same time he received a memo from a former executive-assistant setting out the arguments *against* a fall election. The main point on this side was that there was no issue about which the public was excited, for it would not be concerned with the government's desire for a parliamentary majority. Pearson's original inclination was not to have an election, and he drafted a statement to that effect for a party strategy meeting. However, a colleague swayed him by saying that he was letting his personal dislike of election campaigns influence his views. He succumbed to the arguments that the government could accomplish its goals, free from Opposition harrassment, if it had a majority in Parliament, and he believed that an election victory would be a public vindication of his integrity after the buffeting he had taken during the recent scandals. Pearson went on national television on September 7, 1965, to announce that a general election would be held on November 8. 'My decision', he said, 'had to be made in the knowledge that we are now facing, in Canada, issues and problems of great importance to our country's future. The country needs a strong central government to deal with these problems, and a stable House of Commons with a majority supporting the Government.'

The Liberal party's political advisers had learned by experience that Pearson was no match for John Diefenbaker on the hustings. They decided therefore to project the image of a leader who was 'above politics' and concerned primarily with governing the country. The party strategists—Tom Kent, Walter Gordon, and Keith Davey—decided that Pearson should spend fully half the campaign in Ottawa and concentrate on short tours only. Television commercials were to consist of informal discussions to capitalize on his ability to charm small groups, for it was clear that Pearson had no flair with mass audiences. Unfortunately for the Liberal strategists, the 1960s marked the advent of the era of 'personality politics' in North America. Especially after John Kennedy's election as President of the United States in 1960, the public in both Canada and the United States began to look for political leaders with an exciting and attractive personality. Pearson, despite an intense concern for the goals he was trying to

Pearson campaigning in Blind River, Sask., 1965.

achieve, was rarely able to communicate any passion to an audience.

Nor could Pearson explain his fundamental social goals and achievements in a way that excited the public. Despite a legislative record that was, by 1968, very impressive, 70 per cent of Canadians interviewed in March 1968 could not think of anything beneficial that the Pearson government had accomplished. In 1965, with Parliament's having been occupied with various crises and the flag debate during most of his government's first two years in power, there was much more justification for such an attitude. Only in Québec did the Liberal campaign generate any excitement, for there two of Pearson's Cabinet colleagues had succeeded in convincing three impressive newcomers to run as Liberal candidates. The best known of the three was Jean Marchand, a popular union leader. But Marchand had refused to seek election unless the Liberals also offered constituency nominations to two of his friends. One was a prominent journalist, Gérard Pelletier, and the other a little-known law professor and writer by the name of Pierre Elliott Trudeau. Soon referred to as the 'three wise men' from Québec, Marchand, Pelletier, and Trudeau were shortly to play major roles in Ottawa.

John Diefenbaker, for his part, took great delight in ridiculing the government for the recent scandals and embarrassments it had experienced. 'It was on a night such as this,' he told audience after audience, 'that Rivard went out to water the rink.' The line never failed to bring roars of laughter. At other times his attacks were less humorous. 'A vote for this Government,' he said, 'is a vote for an open season for organized crime in Canada.' At one point Diefenbaker's emphasis on the scandals became so great that Pearson felt obliged to devote a telecast to the subject. 'The facts are,' he pointed out, 'first, that the attempt to influence justice failed completely; and, second, that the Government immediately servered connection with the people whose behaviour was questionable ... The rest is insinuation and misrepresentation.' Nevertheless Diefenbaker's constant references to the scandals reinforced Pearson's public image as a weak leader.

In sharp contrast to the Prime Minister, who visited only thirty-two communities during the campaign, Diefenbaker crossed the country in an exhausting train tour that took him to 196 different localities. As he had done in previous campaigns, he demonstrated an instinctive ability to communicate with ordinary people. But while he effectively undermined the government's credibility through ridicule and invective, he was unable to convince the voters that he was a credible alternative. A letter to the Montreal *Star* summed up the frustration felt by many voters: 'Sir. Diefenbaker is impossible. Pearson is irresponsible. Douglas is impractical. Thompson is unbelievable. Caouette is incredible. What shall I do?'

For the most part the electorate was apathetic and indifferent to the election campaign, Canada's fifth in nine years. The issue of the need for majority government was not one that excited the voters; besides, many believed, pointing to the St Laurent government of the 1950s, that majority governments were lethargic and arrogant. Regional and even local issues seemed to predominate in spite of the best efforts of the party leaders to focus attention on national questions. Neither the Liberals' proposals for a national medicare program, tax reform, and new tax-sharing arrangements with the provinces, nor the Conservatives' call for a Royal Commission on Organized Crime and the abolition of the 11-per-cent sales tax on building materials, aroused much interest.

At the outset of the campaign, polls indicated that some 48 per cent of the public favoured the Liberals while only 28 per cent supported the Progressive Conservatives. Liberal strategists were privately predicting that they would win between 140 and 145 seats. But as the election results began to flow in on November 8, the Liberals found to their dismay and shock that they were going to form another minority government. John Diefenbaker's energetic coast-to-coast campaign had succeeded in reducing the Liberals' lead from 20 per cent at the beginning of the campaign to just 7 per cent on election night. The Liberals gained a mere two seats for a total of 131, two short of the magic number that would have given them an over-all majority. The Conservatives gained two for a total of 97, and the NDP picked up four for a total of 21 seats. The Créditistes suffered the biggest losses of all, dropping from 24 to nine members. Social Credit elected five members, and there were two independents. The fact that 223 of the 265 seats did not change hands, the smallest seat turnover in any election since Confederation, suggested that the public had not been stirred by the campaign.

At the Château Laurier in Ottawa, where Liberal officials were watching the returns on television, the atmosphere was one of shock. Finally, at 11:30 p.m., Pearson emerged from his private suite and made a television statement. He said only that the Liberals had by far the largest group in the House of Commons and that it was their responsibility to carry on, although he would not make a final decision until he had had time to assess the situation.

In fact Pearson was much more discouraged than his buoyant appearance on election night indicated. He said later that he had never felt so depressed in his entire political career, for all his hard work seemed to have been for nothing. The prospect of another minority government, subject to the constant danger of defeat in the House of Commons and unable to ensure passage of its legislative program, was a dismal one. After eight years as leader of the Liberal party, Pearson believed that it was time to resign and let the party choose another leader who would be more successful. His feeling of depression did not last long, however. There was still much to be accomplished, his advisers and friends argued, and their appeal was effective. Pearson abandoned his plans to retire immediately, although he did promise his wife (who continued to make no secret of her dislike of his political career) that he would retire within three years, when he reached the age of seventy. For the time being there was still a government to lead.

6

Prime Minister: 1965~8

With the end of another rigorous election campaign (which was to be his last), and having determined to continue as Prime Minister, Pearson settled back into his daily routine. After a light breakfast he would be driven from his residence overlooking the Ottawa River along Sussex Drive to his office in the East Block of the Parliament Buildings. He often listened to the 8 a.m. CBC radio news in the car and arrived at his office around 8:15. After forty-five minutes of solitary work he would meet with his top advisers to discuss the latest developments and his schedule for the day. He often had lunch at his desk, while reading Cabinet documents or preparing for the daily question period if the House was in session. By 6:30 he would be on his way home, barring any last-minute crises, carrying a briefcase filled with several hours' work—usually position papers to study and contemplate. 'More than anything else,' wrote Bruce Hutchison, 'the tedious homework of a born student was the secret of Pearson's success.' Pearson's favourite evenings were spent in front of the television set watching sports programs or westerns. Despite—or perhaps because of—his diplomatic background, he did not participate in the dinner-party circuit that was official Ottawa's chief social activity. His tastes remained simple and his life-style unsophisticated.

Like many others who had graduated from Oxford in the 1920s, Pearson liked bow ties and he wore one often during his diplomatic career. Once he entered political life, however, he was told by his advisers that the bow tie projected an outdated image. But newspaper cartoonists almost always pictured him with one, even though as Prime Minister he wore one infrequently, for they were his trademark and there was little in his physical appearance they could use to caricature. He was of average height and weight—five feet 9 inches, 175 pounds—with hazel eyes and thinning grey hair. He had a youthful appearance, even in middle age, although during his years as Prime Minister he grew noticeably older and seemed to put on weight. When he spoke in the House of Commons he usually stood with his notes in his left hand and his right stuffed into his trousers pocket—he had the rumpled look of an elderly university professor—and when he wished to stress a point his hand chopped the air in short strokes. His impact as a speaker was never very effective—except when he spoke to small groups or specialized audiences, to whom he conveyed an air of sincerity and charm with his quiet sense of humour.

One of Pearson's frustrations was his inability to speak French well. Like many English Canadians, the importance of learning French had not been impressed upon him at school, and he had studied German in high school because the teacher was less demanding. Although he was able to read French fairly well, he always felt slightly humiliated by his inability to speak fluently to French audiences. He could read from a text without too much difficulty, even if his accent was, as he was told on one occasion, 'cute, like a Frenchman speaking in Brooklyn English.' He particularly regretted his inability to speak with Quebeckers on a relaxed, informal basis, which meant that he had to rely on French-

Official portrait of Pearson as Prime Minister, 1965.

THE OLD SMOOTHIE

*Duncan Macpherson's famous cartoon of Pearson,
which appeared in the Toronto* Star *in April 1964.*

speaking Members of Parliament and advisers for an assessment of the situation in Québec.

Pearson's decision-making techniques reflected his own strengths and limitations. He was not an innovative thinker and had few specific objectives of his own. His talents lay in taking theoretical ideas suggested by others and building a practical policy from them. He would listen to a wide variety of opinions expressed by Cabinet ministers or officials without stating his own views. Once they had left he would usually pick up the telephone and discuss the matter with a variety of informed contacts whose judgement he respected. Judy LaMarsh, one of Pearson's Cabinet colleagues, wrote in her memoirs: 'He probably had the solicited and unsolicited advice of more prominent, knowledgeable people in all walks of life, both within and without Canada, and particularly of national and international public servants and members of the academe, than any other Prime Minister.' His notable ability to reconcile different points of view, and his willingness to alter his own position if necessary, contributed to the government's image of indecisiveness. Instead of adopting a policy and defending it against all attackers, Pearson was quite prepared to make changes if he was persuaded that the result would be better, or more acceptable. For the most part this approach led to good, well-prepared legislation, but it was carried out so gradually that the public was often unaware of what the government was accomplishing.

One of the ironies of Pearson's period as Prime Minister was that, while he never inspired in the electorate sufficient confidence and trust to be given a majority government, he was loved by the people who knew him or had direct contact with him. As Patrick Nicholson put it, Pearson did not possess Arthur Meighen's towering intellect, or Mackenzie King's adroit political shrewdness, or R. B. Bennett's administrative capability, or Louis St Laurent's dignified aloofness from partisan politics, or John Diefenbaker's gift of compelling oratory. 'But he perhaps had a more winsome quality: immense personal charm. As a likeable man, warm, witty and indeed lovable, Lester Pearson towered above those five predecessors. This characteristic, however, cannot permeate television's picture tube nor the hustings' microphone; so the electors never acquired that loyalty and trust which led his parliamentary supporters to stick with him through tribulation and embarrassment.' Several years later Denis Smith, the biographer of Walter Gordon, concluded that it was Pearson's 'congenial personality' that was his chief political resource, for it created strong bonds of loyalty in a party that had few other unifying ties, and minimized his faults and failures.

In small groups Pearson was instantly able to put people at ease with some sports gossip or a quip, usually self-deprecating. His actions were marked by humility and a lack of selfishness and ambition. His tolerance of men's weaknesses was a source of his inner strength. He could rarely bring himself to hate anyone. When one colleague was known to be plotting against him, he remarked: 'Oh well, everyone knows poor old so-and-so. He can't help it.' In response to criticism that he was not ruthless enough to fire Cabinet ministers who had made mistakes, Pearson replied by describing Mackenzie King's approach: 'When Mr King decided that the time had come for a Cabinet minister to go, he went. But Mr King kept a lot of ministers in his cabinet, I think quite rightly, who had made mistakes and turned out to be even better ministers after they had made the mistakes.' Many of his actions and attitudes were based on his belief in the Christian ethics he had learned as a youth, even though he no longer attended church regularly, having fallen out of the habit during his many foreign postings. 'It was Pearson's sincerity,' commented one MP, 'his lack of deceit, his openness, which made him so popular with the backbenchers. . . . Also, he always found time to talk to us, while most ministers claimed they were too busy.'

However, Pearson was never able to acquire the partisan instinct that facilitates and simplifies a politician's life. As a good diplomat he recognized that issues were not just black or white, that there were shades of right and wrong, and that his party did not have a monopoly on wisdom. One small example of this attitude was his decision that the portraits of both John A. Macdonald and Wilfrid Laurier would be displayed in his East Block office. Previous Liberal prime ministers had hung only the picture of Laurier—Macdonald was relegated to the basement—and Conservative leaders had done the opposite. Pearson's lack of experience with partisan politics often caused him to accept too readily suggestions from his advisers that later proved embarrassing, such as his call for John Diefenbaker's resignation after the 1957 election. Equally damaging was his failure to anticipate Opposition criticism on issues he regarded as unimportant but on which the Opposition was able to embarrass the government. He detested the over-simplified speeches he had to make, although his antipathy towards John Diefenbaker gradually lessened this reluctance. Furthermore his instinctive distrust of partisanship was often overcome by political realities that he could not, or would not, ignore. He was widely criticized for his Senate appointments, which in almost every case went to past or present Liberal members or supporters. Pearson later recalled that he had once been quite idealistic and had hoped to make the Senate into a non-partisan chamber, but decided that this would require a constitutional change. 'The men I appointed to the Senate,' he rationalized not too convincingly, 'were all men of ability and achievement outside politics.'

Pearson's first task following the 1965 election was to reorganize his Cabinet and advisory staff in an attempt to revitalize the government and present a better image. Walter Gordon, who had been most responsible for urging the Prime Minister to call the election, offered his resignation and was replaced as Finance Minister by Mitchell Sharp, a long-time civil servant who had run for Parliament in 1962 because of his liking for Pearson. Jean Marchand, the promising newcomer from Québec, was made Minister of Manpower, and a well-known businessman and former minister, Robert Winters, became Minister of Trade and Commerce. Several other ministers switched portfolios as the government prepared to meet the House in January.

Pearson hoped that 1966 would be a year of recovery for the government, one in which it could concentrate on useful legislation and forget the scandals and controversies of the past. By March, however, it was in the midst of the worst scandal of all. In June the Lesage government was defeated in Québec and replaced by a more truculent, nationalistic one led by Daniel Johnson; and in December the government was forced to raise taxes in order to ease the inflationary problem that was playing havoc with the economy. For Pearson it was a year in which he lost all taste for politics and began to look forward to his retirement with greater enthusiasm than ever.

The first controversy to face the government involved a Vancouver postal clerk named George Victor Spencer. In 1965 the RCMP discovered a Soviet spy ring in Ottawa. Two Russian agents were expelled from the country and the government announced that an unnamed civil servant had been paid thousands of dollars by the Soviets to assist in their espionage operations. Pearson told the House that the civil servant would probably not be charged since he was thought to be dying of cancer. Later, however, a newspaper reporter learned Spencer's identity, and the Minister of Justice told a television interviewer that, although Spencer had not been charged with or convicted of any criminal offence, he had been fired from his job and would be kept under surveillance by the RCMP. Conservative and NDP members were upset that Spencer should have been treated in this manner without a trial and urged that a full inquiry into the case be conducted. Pearson, whose own inclinations were that the inquiry should be held, was persuaded by the RCMP and his colleagues that an appeal would endanger the RCMP's sources of information and methods of operation in cases involving national security. Besides, Pearson was convinced that Spencer had been fairly treated. The Opposition's cause was aided, however, when Spencer himself said that he would like a hearing into his pension situation. Pearson concluded that, since the inquiry would deal only with details concerning his pension rights and would not endanger the RCMP's security operations, the government would be wise to reverse its original decision. Pearson said he would take full responsibility for the change in position by making the announcement himself. Justice Minister Cardin, however, felt obliged to resign since he had been the minister most identified with the government's original decision not to allow an inquiry. Cardin was eventually persuaded to stay on, but not before there was a near-revolt in the Liberal party's Québec caucus, which felt that the Prime Minister had betrayed his Minister of Justice.

Despite some arguments that Pearson's change in policy

had been an act of courage and humanity, it was more widely interpreted as a sign of weakness. The Toronto *Telegram* called for his resignation, charging that Pearson had 'lost control of Parliament and of his Cabinet'. Montreal's *Le Devoir* said that he had shown 'in serious circumstances an astonishing lack of courage', and predicted that he would resign within three months. Pearson's supporters, who seemed to be declining in number, could only argue that the government had treated Spencer as leniently as possible, had not pressed charges since technically he could not be charged under the Official Secrets Act, and had then acceded to his request for an inquiry to improve his pension position.

The Spencer case led to the worst scandal of all: the Munsinger affair. Shortly after the Rivard affair became public in 1964, Pearson had asked the RCMP if they had information of any 'impropriety' involving any Member of Parliament of any party during the previous ten years. (He later justified this request on the grounds that he wanted to compare his handling of the MPs involved in the Rivard case with the way in which other public figures had been dealt with. The Opposition, however, accused him of trying to find information about members of the Diefenbaker government in order to embarrass the Conservative party.) The RCMP informed Pearson that at least one member of the Diefenbaker government, Associate Defence Minister Pierre Sévigny, had been involved with an East-German prostitute and convicted spy, Gerda Munsinger. Because Sévigny had access to military information and his relationship was with a possible Communist agent, the RCMP had informed Prime Minister Diefenbaker, who had apparently instructed Sévigny to end the relationship. During the Rivard scandal, when the Liberal government was being accused of impropriety some ministers were sorely tempted to use the

Munsinger case to embarrass the Conservatives, or at least to threaten them with release of the information if they did not ease up on their attack. Pearson insisted later that he had urged his ministers not to raise the Munsinger issue, although he admitted that it had often been very tempting to do so, especially when Conservative attacks against him frequently appeared unjustified.

During the stormy Commons debate over the Spencer case, John Diefenbaker unloaded a bitter attack on Justice Minister Cardin, accusing him of 'evasion, delusion and deception'. Cardin, visibly upset, pointed to Diefenbaker and said: 'Of all the members he, I repeat he, is the very last person who can afford to give advice on the handling of security cases in Canada.' The Justice Minister then blurted out a reference to the Munsinger case. Several days later Cardin held a press conference at which he intended to announce that he would not, after all, resign because of the Spencer case. Pearson warned him beforehand to make no further reference to Mrs Munsinger and Cardin assured him that he would not. But the Justice Minister, still feeling the sting of Diefenbaker's attacks against him, unleashed a string of accusations. He said that Mrs Munsinger had been engaged in espionage activities before coming to Canada and that her association with Conservative Cabinet ministers had constituted a security risk. When the Conservatives accused the Liberals of deliberate 'muckraking', Pearson could not help feeling that they were getting some of their own medicine. In a private memo Pearson wrote: 'My own criticism of Cardin for the way he has provoked this sensation, with all its private scandals and its effect on Parliament's and Canada's good name, is not, however, total. I would be a hypocrite if I pretended it was, because I believe the ultimate end will justify the dubious means if it gets Diefenbaker and his type out of politics, out of public life.' It was a display of anger that was uncharacteristic of Pearson, showing the depth of his animosity towards his arch political foe.

A riotous series of debates rocked and degraded Parliament for the next two weeks. A Toronto reporter found Gerda Munsinger in Germany and the press rushed to interview her. Pearson, struggling to maintain control of Parliament, proposed the establishment of a judicial inquiry, which eventually concluded that Prime Minister Diefenbaker had erred in not dismissing Sévigny from the Cabinet. In the House the Conservatives moved a non-confidence motion, condemning the government for its inquiry into the past conduct of Members of Parliament. The Toronto *Star* commented the next day that the motion questioned the personal integrity of Prime Minister Pearson, but that the majority of MPs did not doubt his integrity, even if they criticized his methods or policies. The bitter debate that raged through Parliament discredited all members. 'I have never felt,' wrote Judy LaMarsh, 'anything like the atmosphere of raw emotion engendered by the Munsinger debate and the anger, fear, and revulsion of members on all sides. Members scuttled from the House heads down, even though the drama lured them back to their seats as the lethal verbal slashing went on. They were sick, Parliament was sick, but the press had a field day.'

During this period Pearson again came very close to resigning. He later recalled that the series of scandals was his worst memory of political life, and that he often reproached himself for not having been able to control the situation. 'I felt furiously indignant at the unfairness, as I felt it to be, of the muckraking tactics of some members of the opposition and subsequently allowed my emotions to influence my judgement. In such situations I am both too naive and too sensitive, and I feel I didn't exercise the control in the House of Commons that a Prime Minister should have done when facing those circumstances.' Many of his supporters thought this was too harsh a self-indictment, but it indicated his great frustration and revulsion over the Munsinger affair.

Throughout the period 1965-8 the major foreign-policy issues in which Canada was involved concerned its relations with the United States. In January 1965 Pearson and Paul Martin, the Secretary of State for External Affairs, flew to President Johnson's ranch in Texas, where, on an old picnic table in front of the ranch house, the two leaders signed the Canada – U.S. Automotive Agreement. The 'auto pact', as it came to be called, provided for duty-free trade in automotive products between the two countries. It resulted in a large increase in automotive production in Canada and in Canadian exports to the United States, both of which greatly stimulated the Canadian economy. Critics, however, charged that the agreement was a further example of the government's 'continentalist' attitude, by which they meant that the Canadian economy was becoming too reliant on that of the United States. Pearson described the auto pact as 'one of the most important accords ever signed between our two countries in the trade field.' His visit to the President's ranch was enlivened by one incident that Pearson later enjoyed recalling. As Johnson greeted Pearson on his arrival, he inadvertently referred to him as 'Mr Wilson', who was then Prime Minister of Great Britain. Pearson did not mention the slip to his host. Later the two men were watching television in the ranch house when the incident was replayed on the news, much to Johnson's embarrassment.

Cordial relations between the two countries were somewhat strained by two other issues. Walter Gordon's 1965 budget provided that advertising in foreign-owned newspapers and periodicals would no longer be tax-deductable in order to encourage advertisers to support Canadian publications. The American government supported the U.S. publishers' demand that the Canadian editions of *Time* and *Reader's Digest* be excluded from these provisions. There were rumours that the U.S. had threatened that Congressional approval of the auto pact would be endangered if Canada did not agree to the exemption. Gordon took the threat seriously, although Pearson insisted he was unaware of any such threat. Eventually both U.S. publications were granted the exemption they sought and Canadian nationalists were given more ammunition for their charges that the Pearson government was not sufficiently 'independent' of the United States.

A somewhat similar controversy arose in 1966 when the U.S. State Department lobbied on behalf of the Mercantile Bank, an American subsidiary. The Canadian government had decided to restrict non-Canadian ownership of any chartered bank to 25 per cent in order to prevent the expansion in Canada of U.S. banks such as Mercantile, which, it was feared, might otherwise dominate Canada's banking system. Several Cabinet ministers, led by Walter Gordon, insisted that the government remain firm, and a compromise was finally reached that basically maintained the provisions of the government's original policy. Canadian nationalists were happier this time, and Canadian-American relations were only temporarily upset by the incident.

The involvement of the United States in the war in Vietnam was becoming increasingly unpopular in Canada by 1967, and the Canadian government was subjected to growing criticism for selling arms to the U.S., some of which were eventually used in Vietnam. Canada was a member of a supervisory commission that had been established in Vietnam in 1954 but was powerless to bring about a cease-fire. The government sent its chief representative on the commission to Hanoi in an attempt to assess the prospects for peace and to convey a message to North Vietnam from the U.S., but neither side seemed interested in a cease-fire. In April 1965, as public criticsm over U.S. bombing raids on North Vietnam was increasing, Pearson decided on his own initiative to suggest a pause in the bombing. In a speech at Temple University in Philadelphia he stated there was a possibility that a pause in the air strikes might provide North Vietnam's leaders with an opportunity to begin peace negotiations, since they would then not appear to be giving in to American military pressure. Pearson flew from Philadelphia to Camp David, where he was coldly received by President Johnson. Several Canadian newspapers, while agreeing with the content of Pearson's speech, questioned the wisdom of his delivering it while in the United States, for they pointed out that Canadians would be upset if an American visitor criticized Canadian government policy. Furthermore, unknown to Pearson, Johnson had been contemplating just the bombing suspension Pearson had proposed. Now the President was reluctant to take such action since it might appear to have been dictated by foreign pressure. In Canada Pearson succeeded in reducing the criticism that he had done nothing to try to end the war in Vietnam, but his ill-timed intervention contributed to the unsettled state of Canadian – American relations without helping the situation in Vietnam.

One area in which Pearson was more successful was the Commonwealth. The granting of independence in the late 1950s and early 1960s to a large number of former British colonies in Africa was rapidly transforming the Common-wealth from a predominantly white institution (dominated by Britain, Canada, Australia, and New Zealand) into one in which African and Asian states were in the majority. But this transformation was accompanied by tensions that threatened to split the Commonwealth along racial lines and bring about its demise. In 1964 Canada won the admiration of the 'non-white' members of the Commonwealth by playing a leading role in the drafting of a declaration that established the principle of racial equality among member-countries. Lionel Chevrier, as Canada's High Commissioner to Britain, had an opportunity to observe Pearson in action at one of the Commonwealth conferences. 'Pearson', he wrote, 'was marvellous at such meetings. He moved among the prime ministers with ease and had the confidence of them all. His interventions in the debate were always timely and carefully listened to. For some reason or other, he seemed always to come down on the right side of a question and thereby gain the confidence of the Asian and African heads of govern-ment, while colleagues of the so-called white Commonwealth often seemed to come down on the wrong side.' The greatest problems came in 1965, when the British colony of Rhodesia unilaterally declared its independence and announced its intention to maintain a white-dominated government. African nations insisted that Britain set a fixed date for a constitu-tional conference that would lead towards majority govern-ment. Pearson was credited with averting a major Common-wealth split when he convinced the African leaders that they should not do anything that would tie Britain's hands in the negotiations. At the January 1966 conference of Common-wealth Heads of Government, held in Lagos, Nigeria, Pearson again helped resolve differences by proposing that, if economic sanctions against Rhodesia failed, an appeal for action should be made to the United Nations. It was one of the rare occasions when Pearson, as Prime Minister, had an opportunity to use abroad the diplomatic talents that had won him fame as Canada's foreign minister. As he drove past smiling crowds in Lagos, Pearson could not help reflecting on the results of the 1965 election: 'It's too bad they couldn't have voted last November or I'd have made it by a mile.'

Canada's other successful foreign-policy initiatives were few and far between. In 1966, after being presented with the Atlantic Award for his efforts to promote co-operation among countries of the North Atlantic, Pearson called for changes in NATO, which, he still believed, had to become more than a military alliance if it was to survive and remain useful. But his call for 'common, unifying political institutions . . . and economic policies' went unheeded. In 1966 Canada began to move away from its opposition to the admission of the People's Republic of China to the United Nations and abstained on the vote in the General Assembly. As with its other efforts to reform the United Nations, however, this one did not succeed, at least at the time. The international environment was less favourable for the kind of initiatives Canada had taken in the 1950s.

Pearson and his Cabinet had barely had time to recover from the disappointing 1965 election results when they were faced with another major challenge from Québec. The carefully constructed policy of co-operative federalism, which had seemed to be on the road to success after the pension-plan agreement in 1964, began to break down early in 1966. In January Premier Lesage, feeling the pressure from nationalists in the province, withdrew his support for a formula that would have enabled Canada to revise its own constitution without the formal approval of Great Britain. This could not be done without the agreement of all the provinces, and Lesage's policy reversal was a heavy blow to the spirit of trust that lay behind the theory of co-operative federalism.

In its 1966 Speech from the Throne, the Québec government announced its intention to gain complete control over the field of social security. From the federal government's point of view, this was a challenge to the principle that Ottawa had the responsibility to set minimum standards across the country for such benefits as family allowances. A further complication was Québec's growing involvement in international activities, which were traditionally regarded as the responsibility of the federal government. After Québec had negotiated a number of cultural and exchange agreements with France in fields of provincial jurisdiction, the Pearson government signed an 'umbrella agreement' with France that allowed Québec to negotiate such agreements. This 'accord-cadre' was more than a face-saving device for Ottawa. The federal government became increasingly concerned that if Québec were allowed to act as an independent government in its relations with other countries, the door would be open for its separation from Confederation.

The conflict deepened and assumed a new dimension when the Lesage government was defeated in June 1966 by Daniel Johnson and his Union Nationale party. Despite his English surname, Johnson was a more ardent Québec nationalist than Lesage. He wanted not only financial but also constitutional changes. Johnson set out his ideas in a book with the threatening title *Equality or Independence.* He said that Québec should remain part of Canada only if it were given equal status in an 'associate state' arrangement, with the other nine provinces together. While other provinces sympathized with some of Québec's financial demands. Premier Johnson's strident constitutional demands aroused renewed fears that Québec was moving in the direction of separatism.

The response of the Pearson government to these changing conditions—in sharp contrast to its earlier emphasis on co-operative federalism—was to become more firm. In March 1966 Pearson delivered the keynote speech at a Liberal gathering in Québec City. He emphasized the need for a strong federal government that respected provincial rights and insisted that he was going to carry out his obligations to his country. His fighting speech prompted a Montreal *Star* reporter to observe that 'Lester Pearson's position within his own government and party is stronger than at any time since he became its leader and took office in 1963.' On another occasion he stated that the federal government had shown its good faith with Québec, but that there could be no more federal adaptability to provincial requirements 'unless there is the conviction that every province wishes to see a strong confederation with a strong central government discharging the powers given to it by the constitution.' At two federal-provincial conferences in the fall the federal government adopted such a firm position that the participants were unable to agree on a final communiqué. The provinces accepted reluctantly a two-year test period for new equalization and shared-cost programs.

The main reason for the government's hardening attitude was the advice Pearson was receiving from the three new MPs who had been elected from Québec in the 1965 election: Jean Marchand, Gérard Pelletier, and especially Pierre Elliott Trudeau. Pearson now found at his side three articulate Quebeckers with very definite and intellectually defined arguments about the best way to treat Québec. Trudeau, who was the main theorist of the three, developed a particularly good relationship with the Prime Minister. He was soon appointed Pearson's parliamentary secretary and spent several evenings in the study of 24 Sussex Drive discussing his ideas with the Prime Minister. Trudeau believed that Québec should be given no special status, for once it was admitted that Québec City was the natural government of French-Canadians, separation was the logical result. What was necessary, he argued, was to convince French Canadians that Ottawa could protect their interests just as well as Québec City. 'We must,' Pearson's speeches began to emphasize, 'make all Canada, and not merely Québec, a homeland for all French Canadians.' An important stride towards this goal was taken in April 1966 when the Prime Minister announced that steps would be taken to increase the bilingual capacity of the civil service in Ottawa. The government believed such a policy was necessary if increasing numbers of French Canadians were to be attracted to work in the federal government; if they could not work in French in Ottawa, it would be only natural for them to regard the federal government as the government of English Canada.

These and other reforms, which some observers credited with halting Québec's drift towards separatism in the late 1960s, aroused strong opposition in English Canada, where the rationale behind them was not well understood. 'The true spirit of Confederation', complained the Calgary *Herald*, 'is in danger of being washed away amid a tide of agitation for such innovations as a bilingual civil service, [and] educational rights for French-speaking minorities in provinces outside of Québec . . . ' Some Ottawa MPs expressed a legitimate fear that the bilingualism proposals would cause hardship for unilingual English-Canadian civil servants if they were applied too rigorously. 'Pretty soon', complained one, 'it'll be compulsory to be bilingual to empty a wastebasket.'

Many of the western complaints were indirectly inspired by the fact that the Pearson government had largely ignored western Canada, just as the Diefenbaker government before it had ignored the aspirations of Québec. Western discontent was more psychological than economic in origin, inspired by a feeling that federal politicians were not interested in the West. As one Cabinet minister, Allan MacEachen, admitted, this feeling was not unjustified: 'In our efforts to rebuild the party after the 1958 defeat, we concentrated on Québec and Ontario. The West became an afterthought.' Pearson was as responsible as anyone for this failure. As he had been raised in Ontario and had spent all his working life in Canada there, it was not surprising that it was to Ontario that his main attention was directed. The multitude of challenges with which he had to deal, especially from Québec, left him little time or energy to undertake new tasks.

The last major federal-provincial confrontation during Pearson's administration was the constitutional conference that was held in February 1968. The main federal spokesman was Pierre Trudeau, whom Pearson had elevated to the Justice portfolio in April 1967. The meeting was stormy at times, for while Trudeau pressed for a guarantee that French-speaking Canadians outside Québec should have the same rights as English-speaking Canadians inside Québec, the Québec government was more concerned with improving its constitutional position. Pearson, as the conference chairman, let Trudeau do most of the speaking but used his diplomatic talents to smooth over difficult moments. Television viewers saw for the first time his ability to defuse a tense moment with

With Pierre Elliott Trudeau, Justice Minister, at the Federal-Provincial Conference of February 1968.

a quip that made everyone laugh and his sense of when a coffee break was needed to prevent an explosive confrontation. 'This was vintage Pearson,' said columnist Charles Lynch. The Ottawa *Citizen* wrote: 'The Canadian people at last have had a chance to see for themselves why Prime Minister Pearson won the Nobel Peace Prize.' Through skilful negotiating the federal government succeeded in gaining provincial acceptance for guarantees of language rights to French Canadians outside Québec. The agreement marked the official beginning of a new approach towards the English-French question in Canada, which was to be continued by its main architect, Pierre Trudeau.

The happiest feature of Pearson's period as Prime Minister was provided by the celebration of Centennial Year, 1967, when Canada marked the one-hundredth anniversary of Confederation, and by the spirit of successful accomplishment and national identity it engendered. Preparations for the various celebrations were the responsibility of the Secretary of State, Judy LaMarsh. One of her tasks was to arrange for various Cabinet ministers to attend the many ceremonies and festivities that were scheduled throughout the year. But she soon found that some ministers were reluctant to commit themselves to attend, for they were not sure whether the celebrations would be a success. Pearson, determined that the year would be a successful one, told her to assign the ministers to whatever functions she wished.

Centennial Year began with a burst of excitement on the snow-covered lawn of Parliament Hill on the evening of December 31, 1966. Prime Minister Pearson lit the Centennial flame, the National Centennial Choir sang a special anthem, and the inevitable speeches were made. As Canadians watched the ceremony on television in their homes across the country, most were gripped by a feeling of patriotism and pride that was to grow and mature throughout the year.

The Department of the Secretary of State had planned many imaginative programs. A Centennial train toured the country with displays that told the story of Canada; canoeists representing each province reversed the path of the original voyageurs in a race that began at Rocky Mountain House in Alberta and ended in Montreal; and communities across the country planned their own centennial projects, with financial assistance from the federal government. These projects ranged from concert halls and community centres to a landing pad for Martian spaceships. A patriotic song, 'Can-a-da', took the country by storm and won a gold record for its composer, Bobby Gimby, who travelled across the country with a Pied Piper costume to lead singing children through the streets. The whole country was caught up in a surge of patriotic excitement that surprised even the most optimistic of the Centennial Year planners.

The focal point of the year was the International Exposition, Expo 67, which was held in Montreal and attracted world-wide publicity for the country. Queen Elizabeth and Prince Philip visited Canada in the summer and were escorted around the exposition grounds by the Prime Minister. Although security officials had vetoed a royal ride on the mini-rail that circled the site, Pearson insisted that it be added to the program, saying he would take full and personal responsibility for anything that might happen. The ride was the highlight of the royal couple's visit to Expo.

Pearson's own centennial-year schedule involved little travelling, for during most of the summer he had to remain in Ottawa to receive the steady stream of foreign leaders who

Prime Minister and Mrs Pearson, with Governor General and Mrs Michener, welcome Queen Elizabeth and Prince Philip as they arrive in Canada to visit Expo 67.

accepted the Canadian government's invitation to visit Canada and Expo 67. Some sixty state visitors were received on Parliament Hill and officially entertained. As a result of the innumerable state dinners that were given for them, Pearson was said to have gained nine pounds in spite of regular exercise on a reducing bicycle.

Although the state visits took place with no major problems, the visit to Canada of French President Charles de Gaulle was an exception. Canadian officials had suspected for some time that the French government was encouraging nationalist and even separatist elements in Québec as part of its plan to enhance the international position of France and the French language. De Gaulle's visit confirmed these fears. After a motorcade from Québec City to Montreal, during which he was warmly applauded, the French President addressed an excited crowd from the balcony of Montreal's city hall. He remarked that during the trip from Québec City he had felt an atmosphere similar to the one he encountered when he entered Paris to liberate it from the Nazis. He concluded by repeating the separaist slogan, 'Vive le Québec libre' (long live free Québec), which the enthusiastic young crowd took up rhythmically.

The Canadian government and most of the country were shocked that an official visitor would blatantly interfere in another country's internal matters. Pearson was especially incensed by the General's reference to the 'liberation'. The next day the Prime Minister appeared on national television and delivered a stinging rebuke to the French President: 'I am sure that Canadians in all parts of our country were pleased when the President of France received such a warm welcome in Québec. However, certain statements by the President tend to encourage the small minority of our population whose aim is to destroy Canada; and, as such, they are unacceptable to the Canadian people and its government. The people of Canada are free. Every province of Canada is free. Canadians do not need to be liberated. Indeed, many thousands of Canadians gave their lives in two world wars in the liberation of France and other European countries. Canada will remain united and will reject any effort to destroy her unity.' The French President, upon learning of the rebuke, decided not to continue on to Ottawa and returned to France immediately. Pearson's reaction was that the general's decision to cut short his visit to Canada was understandable in the circumstances. 'But those circumstances, which are not of the [Canadian] government's making, are greatly to be regretted.' Relations between Canada and France were frigid as long as de Gaulle remained president; they subsequently thawed as the Gaullist influence in the French government diminished.

Centennial Year had a profound effect on Canadians. Accustomed to looking to other countries—Britain, the United States, or France—for political, economic, and cultural ideas, they acquired a new sense of confidence in themselves and in Canada. For many Canadians the strikingly successful Expo 67, and its world-wide fame, was the first convincing evidence they had ever had that Canada could do things every bit as well as other countries. Following upon that festive year, Canadian literature began to grow in popularity and quality; economic nationalism became more widespread as growing numbers of Canadians felt the need for greater control over their own economy; and courses in Canadian studies became more popular in universities. This new self-confidence was not without its dangers, though. Some Canadians became strident and irrational in their nationalism, while others became excessively inward-looking and preoccupied with things Canadian. Nevertheless Centennial Year was a watershed in Canada's development as a nation. While Pearson himself had little to do with the actual projects that stimulated Canadians' dormant pride in their country, the success of Centennial Year was an accomplishment for the government as a whole. The Diefenbaker government also deserved a share of the credit, for it was during its period in office that approval was given to the plans for Expo 67, the brilliant symbol of an exciting and gratifying year.

In spite of this outburst of national pride, the final years of Pearson's administration were frustrating ones. The degrading Munsinger scandal had barely died down in 1966 when the country realized that it was facing severe economic problems. While not of crisis proportions, they reflected badly on the government and dampened the mood of optimism that was created by Centennial Year. Canada's problems were in part a result of the unstable international monetary situation. The British pound was in a precarious position and there were fears that the U.S. dollar would be devalued. Inflation was becoming a serious problem throughout the Western world, and the symptoms were also being felt in Canada. Foreign conditions, however, were not solely to blame. The Pearson government's ambitious program of social legislation resulted in a large increase in federal spending, which added more than 20 per cent to the country's national debt. Finance Minister Gordon had been one of the strongest advocates of bold spending proposals, and many of the government's programs, such as the Canada Pension Plan, were badly needed. However, since the Minister of Finance is usually the person responsible for keeping expenditures within a reasonable limit, the fact that Gordon was such an advocate of increased spending meant that there was no powerful minister during the first years of the Pearson administration who looked with a critical eye at new

proposals. In 1965 Pearson announced a cutback in government spending, realizing that the injection of more and more
money into the economy was having an inflationary effect. But
most Canadians had not realized the need for spending limitations, and in his election program later in the year Pearson was
not prepared to insist upon them. The Toronto *Globe and Mail*
expressed a common reaction to his cutback announcement:
'Canada is not in any mood, and certainly not in any practical
position, to stall development for long. . . . The post-war baby
crop is coming into the market, as workers, as consumers, as
the formers of new family units. Their need for housing, transportation, job opportunities, consumer goods and education
can scarcely be underestimated. Canada must grow or stran-
gle.' With the advent of the November election, Pearson succumbed to temptation and promised the country a wide range
of costly hockey arenas, bridges, and harbours.

By 1966, with the economic situation rapidly worsening,
the government was aware of the need for quick action. In a
rapid succession of budgets the new Finance Minister, Mitchell Sharp, took steps to slow down the country's economic
growth in an attempt to stop the inflationary cycle. The tax
increases he instituted on personal income as well as on
liquor and tobacco were not politically popular, but the government was convinced they were necessary.

The growing danger of inflation, which was becoming serious by 1967, was combined with pressure on the Canadian
dollar and a growing budgetary deficit. The government came
under increasing criticism. A Gallup Poll published in November 1967 showed that 47 per cent of Canadians thought
that Pearson should resign. The Progressive Conservative
party had just elected a new leader, Robert Stanfield, at a
national convention that had provided a great deal of publicity
for the party, and opinion polls showed that he was more popu-

lar than the Prime Minister. Moreover, members of Pearson's Cabinet were already beginning to campaign informally to replace him as party leader, for they knew that he was likely to retire in the near future. A large number of Cabinet leaks embarrassed the government during this time, for several of the leadership candidates wanted their views to be publicized as widely as possible. On several occasions Pearson insisted firmly that what had been discussed at a certain Cabinet meeting was to be kept absolutely secret, only to find the exact details of the discussion—plus his insistence on secrecy—published in newspapers the next day. 'Seldom', wrote columnist Anthony Westell, 'has an administration decayed so fast. With three years of its mandate still to run, the Pearson Cabinet is showing symptoms of disintegration that may be the prelude to collapse.' Although Parliament continued to pass good legislation at a steady pace, in the public's eye the government seemed to be stumbling helplessly from crisis to crisis.

Pearson and his wife Maryon had long before decided that he would retire from political life as close to his seventieth birthday as possible. Since it fell in April 1967, however, Pearson felt he could not resign in the midst of Centennial Year. His resignation would detract from the excitement of the festivities and, besides, he enjoyed the ceremonies in which he was involved and the steady stream of foreign visitors.

In December 1967, at a small family gathering to celebrate his wife's birthday, Pearson gave her the present she had long been waiting for: a firm promise to retire from politics. At that week's regular Cabinet meeting, when the topic of adjustment assistance was about to be discussed, Pearson interrupted the proceedings. 'Speaking of adjustment assistance,' he said, 'I want to read you a letter I've just sent to Senator Nichol', the president of the Liberal Federation. At a press conference a few hours later, he read the letter, which began: 'I wish to inform you of my decision, taken after lengthy and serious consideration, to resign from the Leadership of our Party.' Although he would have liked to relinquish his responsibilities as quickly as possible, he was told that it would take at least four months before a leadership convention could be organized. 'Until the convention has chosen my successor I will, of course, continue to serve as Leader of the Party.'

Asked by a reporter what had been the most satisfying and disappointing moments in his career, Pearson quipped that he did not want to 'scoop' himself, since he planned to write his memoirs after he retired. He added: 'I wouldn't say that my actual introduction to leadership was the high spot of my career. I'm thinking of the day I got up in the House of Commons and moved my first motion. After that I had no place to go but up.' Then, when the questions from the reporters appeared to be over, the retiring Prime Minister shrugged his shoulders and grinned. 'Well, good-bye,' he said. 'C'est la vie.'

During the next four months, while contestants for the leadership began to organize their campaigns. Pearson remained in office. Although some reporters feared that a 'lame-duck' Prime Minister would not be able to command sufficient authority to lead the government effectively, Pearson presided over the February 1968 constitutional conference with great skill. His announced intention to retire enhanced his image as an ideal chairman. While his Justice Minister, Pierre Elliott Trudeau, was the main spokesman for the federal government, Pearson was able to concentrate on mediating the frequent clashes between Trudeau and Québec Premier Daniel Johnson.

Shortly after the constitutional conference the government experienced a major crisis in the House of Commons. On February 19, while Pearson was taking a brief holiday in Jamaica after the strain of the conference, a government bill to impose a surtax on personal incomes was defeated on third reading by two votes, 84-82. This was in large part accidental, resulting from the fact that several Liberal Cabinet ministers were out of town campaigning for the party leadership, while other MPs were spending the Monday evening in their constituencies. Whatever the reason, the fact remained that the government had been defeated in the House and this raised the inevitable question: should it resign?

The conditions under which defeat in the House of Commons required the resignation of the government were unclear, for much of Canada's parliamentary tradition is built on rules and practices that are nowhere written down. The British North America Act, for example, does not even mention the existence of a Prime Minister, and the fact that a Prime Minister is regarded as the country's leader is primarily the result of long-established custom. As for parliamentary defeats, all that custom had determined was that a government was obliged to resign if it was defeated on a vote that was clearly a reflection of the non-confidence of the House; bills involving the expenditure of public money were usually included in this category, since it was in this area that the British House of Commons had originally asserted its primacy over the King. The Conservative party, therefore, called for the government to resign. With the Liberal party in the midst of a leadership race, and having just elected a new leader of their own, the Conservatives realized that they stood an excellent chance of winning the election if they could force one to be called.

Pearson was no less aware of the tremendously hazardous position in which the vote had put his party, not to mention himself. The last thing he wanted, now that he was so close to retirement, was to have to fight another election campaign, especially as a 'lame-duck' leader. Therefore, after his hasty return to Ottawa from his interrupted holiday, he set out to accomplish two goals: convince the Conservatives not to force an election and, above all, persuade the Canadian public that the government should not resign.

His first step was to ask Robert Stanfield, the new Leader of the Opposition, to agree to a twenty-four-hour adjournment of Parliament. It was later suggested that Pearson had convinced Stanfield that the financial problems facing the country were so serious that the country could ill afford another election. Stanfield, whether because of his own sense of responsibility or Pearson's persuasiveness or both, agreed to the adjournment instead of pressing the attack, as John Diefenbaker and several other Conservatives were urging. The delay gave Pearson some breathing space. He soon appeared on national television in an attempt to convince the Canadian public that the government should not resign. He argued that the defeat had been a mere 'hazard of minority government', and that if minority governments were required to resign after every defeat in the House, there would never be a stable Parliament. The vote had not really been one of confidence, he said, since the principle of the bill had been agreed upon at second reading, and third reading was little more than a formality. Pearson's arguments were upheld by some constitutional experts, such as Eugene Forsey, but the scholars were not unanimous.

What mattered most was public opinion, and here the decision seemed clear. Members of Parliament from all parties reported that their constituents simply did not want another election. Members of the minority parties were especially aware of this fact. Two days after the government's defeat in the House, the Prime Minister introduced a motion saying that the defeat had not constituted a real vote of non-confidence in the government. With the support of the Créditistes, the Liberals won the decisive vote, 138-119. There were those who believed that as a result of these events Parliament had lost its important prerogative of being able to defeat a government over a money bill. Others believed that parliamentary traditions were evolving in the only way that was possible if the election of minority governments was not to result in perpetual political instability. As the constitutional experts debated the pros and cons of what the government had done, Pearson heaved an immense sigh of relief. At least he would not have to fight another election campaign.

But while the government had survived, the victory had been costly. The leadership aspirations of Paul Martin (who had been campaigning in Trois-Rivières on the night of the vote) and of Mitchell Sharp (whose responsibility it had been to pilot the bill through the House) had been dealt a damaging blow. The government's image, already suffering from previous scandals, was further weakened. And the situation continued to deteriorate as ministers refused to interrupt their campaigning to attend debates in which their department's estimates or legislation were involved, and as the leaks from Cabinet continued. 'Half the Cabinet', complained one minister later, 'seemed to be out running for office, while the others were importuned to line up behind one or the other aspirant. The Prime Minister appeared to have lost all control.'

Though Pearson's last months in power were anything but the highlight of his career, Canadians began to look on him more fondly as the date of his retirement approached. Whatever might be the assessment of his leadership abilities—and they did not then appear to be highly considered by many—there could be no mistaking his basic human qualities. His charm and his quiet dignity became more apparent than ever as Canadians realized that they were soon to lose a leader whom they had come to admire and respect. The inevitable retirement parties and words of praise followed. Members of his staff presented him with an extension ladder, a saw, a hatchet, and a 'Private property, keep out' sign for his retirement years. The Prime Minister replied that he would now be able to make three dollars an hour doing odd jobs around Rockcliffe (the Ottawa surburb in which he lived).

A week before the leadership convention Pearson made his final appearance at the Parliamentary Press Gallery's annual dinner, where he had in the past won the hearts of the press corps with his talent for making jokes at his own expense. His speech was full of the humour that had made him loved by those who knew him best. At the end he said: 'I do not forgive myself for the occasional refusal—born of obstinacy out of experience—to take the advice of the pundits of the Press Gallery on each issue that arose. I paid for that neglect almost as heavily as I would have if I had done what they advised.

'My sixty days of decision were too decisive. I failed to get three maple leaves on the flag and I lost the blue border . . . I failed to realize that unification of the armed forces should have been preceded by unification of the Cabinet. I was wrong in relying entirely on the Sermon on the Mount as the guidelines for Cabinet solidarity. . . .

'So I leave you, with head held high, chins up, step steady, conscious of a job half-done; confident also that the verdict of history will be: *Après lui, le déluge.*'

The convention to choose a new leader of the Liberal party was held in Ottawa on the weekend of April 4-6. Although most of the attention revolved around the choice of the new leader, the first night of the convention was 'Pearson Night', at which the delegates were given an opportunity to show their appreciation of the man who had guided their party back from political oblivion. As Pearson and his wife entered the coliseum, a thunderous cheer rose from more than 9,000 voices. A swarm of policemen had to push through the human crush to get the Pearsons to the stage. There, bathed in television lights, Pearson lifted his arms above his head as the ovation continued. When the Prime Minister was officially introduced, he was so overwhelmed by the warmth of the reception that he grasped the edge of the podium until his knuckles were white, bowed his head, and let tears fill his eyes. Then he lifted his arms in an attempt to silence the crowd, which was still applauding wildly.

More than a minute later, when the noise had finally died down, Pearson made his last speech as Prime Minister. He began by recalling his words on assuming the party leadership in 1958, when he had said that he would undoubtedly make mistakes but that they would be honest ones for which he would not have to apologize to his conscience. 'Tonight, as I hand back to the party the trust and the honour I received from it that day, I acknowledge, and regret, those promised mistakes, while I am happy and grateful for any good things I have done or good results I have helped to achieve.' Among the achievements, he mentioned particularly the 'new pride in Canada' that had resulted from the introduction of the new flag; government support of the arts; Centennial Year; and efforts to create a more co-operative form of federalism. Then for a moment he returned to the interna-

*Prime Minister and Mrs Pearson wave farewell
to an enthusiastic crowd at the Civic Centre in
Ottawa, the night of Pearson's retirement as
leader of the Liberal party, April 4, 1968.*

tionalist theme that had dominated his thinking throughout his life. 'The last thing we Canadians should do is to shut ourselves up in our provinces, or, indeed, in our own country or our own continent. If we are to be of service in the world and to ourselves . . . we must look beyond our own national or local limits. Our foreign policy must remain based on this principle.' Finally he spoke of the problem of national unity. 'So we who believe in our country, and our party as an instrument to serve it, must work with "a passionate intensity" to see that this [Québec separatism] doesn't happen; that the Canadian dream does not end but is realized in a Canadian destiny worthy of those who have brought us so far in our first century.'

Throughout his 30-minute speech, the crowd interrupted him with applause some thirty times. When he sat down, with the words 'Thank you and good-bye', a roar went up from the audience: 'We want Lester! We want Lester!' The crowd called him back to the microphone three times, alternating their rhythmical cry with choruses of 'For he's a jolly good fellow' and 'Il a gagné ses épaulettes'. Finally, when the band struck up 'Auld Lang Syne', emotion in the auditorium reached a peak. Everyone stood and sang while the Pearsons, joined by their son and daughter and their grandchildren, linked arms on stage. It was an emotional evening as the Liberal party—and the millions of Canadians who were watching on television—said good-bye to Mike Pearson.

The next day the overflowing warmth and affection of Pearson Night were forgotten as the delegates began the serious work of electing a new leader. Mitchell Sharp had withdrawn his candidacy a few days earlier, since the country's financial problems had forced him to spend more time in Ottawa than on the campaign trail. He threw his support behind Justice Minister Trudeau, whose youthful image and intellectual flair had caught the imagination of many Canadians. Although Pearson was careful not to express any personal preference in public, few doubted that Pierre Trudeau was also *his* choice. Their evening discussions at 24 Sussex had convinced him that Trudeau had a well-developed philosophy that would enable him to deal with nationalist elements in Québec and to promote national unity. The other main contenders—Robert Winters, Paul Hellyer, and John Turner—not only lacked Trudeau's flair but seemed more conservative in their approach to social and economic policies. When the ballotting was finally over, Pierre Elliott Trudeau was the new leader of the Liberal Party of Canada. Lester Pearson went home with the feeling that his successor had been well chosen.

On the morning of April 20, two weeks after the leadership convention, Pearson made his last public appearance as Prime Minister when he led a 'Miles for Millions' march. On the steps of Parliament he listened as some 25,000 voices joined in a chorus of Happy Birthday. 'You're three days early,' said the Prime Minister, who then proceeded down the steps of the Parliament Buildings and into the surging crowd while the Governor General's Foot Guard Band struck up a march. But Pearson did not walk far. After going about three hundred yards, he waved to the crowd and stepped into his limousine. He had one last task to perform as Prime Minister—to turn the reins of government officially over to Pierre Trudeau.

At 11 a.m. Pearson arrived at Rideau Hall for his appointment with Governor General Michener. There the head of state received his resignation and that of his Cabinet, following which he swore in Pierre Elliott Trudeau as Canada's

fifteenth Prime Minister. After the customary glass of cham-
pagne, Pearson turned to go. Emerging from Rideau Hall
into a swarm of reporters and cameramen, he smiled and told
everyone 'Call me Mike now.' He added that, while his
retirement involved a 'certain regret', he also had 'a real
feeling of relief'. Pearson then made his way through the
newsmen, got into his car and drove home.

That afternoon the Pearsons drove inconspicuously through
Hull on their way to a cottage in the Gatineau hills for their
first weekend in years as private citizens. At night, alone at
the cottage, they watched the hockey game on television and
the next day they sat together in the sun. On April 23
Pearson celebrated a quiet family birthday, and two weeks
later he and Maryon left for a holiday in Ireland. For a man
who had never relished the demands of public life, the prospect ahead was a happy one.

7

The End of a Career: 1968~72

When he announced his intention to resign as leader of the Liberal party in December 1967, Lester Pearson said he planned to retire to his little 'rose-covered cottage' in Rockcliffe. But few people who knew him believed that he would spend his retirement years in tranquil inactivity. The demands that are inevitably put upon a former head of government, combined with Pearson's own energy and his inability to refuse a request to support a good cause, ensured that the years left to him were hardly less active than his life as a diplomat and politician.

His first major activity came in the field of international development assistance. In the fall of 1967, while still Prime Minister, Pearson read a speech by the president of the World Bank, an international organization charged with the onerous task of helping the world's poor countries in Africa, Asia, and Latin America. The president had called for a major study by a group of experts to determine where past aid efforts had failed and what should be done to lessen the huge disparity in wealth that existed among different countries. Pearson thought the project was worthwhile and wrote the president endorsing the idea. When the World Bank decided to undertake the study, it remembered his earlier enthusiasm and interest and asked him to lead the commission. Pearson agreed on two conditions: that he be given complete freedom to choose the commissioners, the supporting staff, and the issues to be studied, and that he be permitted to take his wife on some of the required trips. In August 1968 he assumed his duties as chairman of the Commission on International Development.

During the next year his schedule was as active as it had ever been. To prepare the report, he and the experts he had invited to assist him travelled around the world, holding meetings in Latin America, Africa, Asia, and the Middle East. In a parallel series of consultations, Pearson met with representatives of the developed countries that would be providing the aid. During this period he cut out most of his other commitments and speaking engagements, believing that the need to arouse support for assistance to developing countries was crucially important. Asked why he had accepted the gruelling task of preparing a report on such a complex subject, Pearson replied: 'I accepted because I believe no problem to be more important to the future of the world.'

When the report was published in the fall of 1969 it was hailed as a comprehensive textbook in the field of international development assistance. Its purpose, in Pearson's mind, was to convince donor countries of the need to be more generous with their aid. It therefore presented a persuasive answer to the question of why a country should share its resources with less-developed nations; at the same time it pointed out that international support for foreign aid was declining. It made recommendations in ten major fields, calling for substantially increased levels of assistance by 1975 and suggesting ways in which aid could be put to use more effectively. The theme of the report—that developed and developing countries must work in partnership if development is to succeed— was convincingly and carefully argued. While it had no discernible direct impact on countries' policies, the report was frequently cited during debates on international development and provided substantial ammunition for those in all countries who wanted assistance to be more generous and more effective.

The commission's report was eventually published in several languages other than English, and in many instances its title translated simply as *The Pearson Report*. Pearson had not authorized the use of this title (the report's correct title was *Partners in Development: Report of the Commission on International Development*) and was embarrassed by it; he reluctantly withdrew his opposition when he learned that the word 'partners' was almost impossible to translate in many languages. The head of the commission's staff, Edward Hamilton, wrote afterwards that the report was in fact Pearson's—'not because he wrote it but because it is difficult to imagine how it could have been done without him.' Pearson left almost all of the actual writing to his staff and did not even rule on contentious issues as they were being decided, for he recognized that other members of the commission had greater technical expertise in this field. He performed instead—as he had done throughout his career—a basically catalytic function. Hamilton later wrote: 'Pearson specialized in the *process* of getting the public business done. Having established the general directions in which movement is desired, he became highly skilled at the subtle business of easing, nursing, inching the ponderous, often hostile instruments of government forward.' He did this with a well-developed sense of timing; he knew when to push for an agreement, when to yield gracefully, and when to ease the tension of a meeting with a quip. Hamilton concluded that Pearson's greatest asset was his own fundamental humanity, which brought out the best in those he dealt with: 'His mere presence induced a breath-taking reduction in the pettiness, the self-serving, the back-biting, the callousness, and the small-mindedness to which all of us are subject.'

Once the report was concluded, Pearson was asked to make one more contribution in the field of development assistance. In 1970 the Canadian government established the International Development Research Centre, designed to conduct research into the problems facing developing countries. While most of its funds were to be provided by Canada, the Centre's governors were to be chosen from other countries as well. Pearson was asked to become the first chairman of the Board of Governors of the IDRC, and it was a request he could hardly refuse. While still Prime Minister he had embarked on the preliminary planning for such an institution, and his World Bank report had specifically called on donor countries to set aside money for research projects in the field of international development. In October 1970 Pearson accepted the chairmanship, a position he held until his death.

During this time Pearson also returned to his first profession: university teaching. After his retirement from political life he received many offers from prestigious universities around the world but, preferring to remain in Ottawa, he chose to give a course at Carleton University, a relatively new institution but one that at that time had the only school of international affairs in Canada. Pearson gave one three-hour seminar every week, emphasizing major international events in which he had been personally involved: the decline of the League of Nations, the formation of the United Nations, the Korean War, the Palestine and Suez crises, and peace-keeping activities in the Congo and Cyprus. He gave his course a loose structure and ran the seminar with as little discipline as he had run the Cabinet. The course was understandably popular among the university's graduate students, who had to fight to be admitted to it. Instead of the formal, dignified ex-Prime Minister that many had expected, they found a relaxed, casual, humorous professor with whom they immediately felt at ease. Sitting around a small conference table, the students listened as Pearson gave his impressions and reminiscences about various events; they then peppered him with questions, which he seemed to delight in fielding. Most were left with the impression that he would have made a very good university professor—particularly successful in relating to students, if not perhaps a brilliant scholar—had he not chosen another career.

Pearson began his weekly seminars at Carleton in the fall of 1969, one year later than originally planned because of his extensive World Bank duties. A few months before the beginning of his second academic term, the Trudeau government released the results of its review of Canadian foreign policy, which appeared to criticize Canada's previous emphasis on peace-keeping and its 'honest broker' role. Pearson interpreted this as a criticism of his own conduct of Canada's foreign affairs. He particularly resented the policy-papers' description of Canadian diplomacy under his administration as 'helpful fixing'. To vent his anger, he took his students through a step-by-step account of the major events in Canadian foreign policy, beginning with the signing of the Treaty of Versailles and ending with the growth of Canadian policy towards franco-phone Africa, emphasizing throughout the need for Canada to adopt an outward-looking attitude towards the rest of the world. As it gradually became apparent that Prime Minister Trudeau's foreign policy was not going to differ much in substance from his own, Pearson felt that the wisdom of his approach had been confirmed. When Trudeau engaged in a major diplomatic effort to preserve the unity of the Commonwealth at the 1971 Heads of Government meeting in Singapore and sent his special assistant to meet with various Commonwealth leaders, Pearson joked that he was going to write a letter to the editor of the *Globe and Mail* , complaining about all of Trudeau's 'helpful fixing'. Never in his most ambitious moments, he added, had he contemplated sending his own special assistant on diplomatic missions around the world!

As an elder statesman—for that was how he had come to be regarded—Pearson was offered and accepted a number of honorary positions. Most reflected his long concern with international affairs. In 1968 he became the honorary president of the Institute or Strategic Studies, a London-based disarmament and defence research centre, and in 1970 he accepted a similar position with the World Federalists of Canada. In 1969 he became Chancellor of Carleton University. As with his IDRC position, he took his duties seriously and was anything but a figurehead. Not all his new positions were as lofty. Some reflected another of Pearson's passions—sports. He became the honorary chairman of the board of directors of the Ottawa Rough Riders of the Canadian Football League, and—an appointment that particularly pleased him—honorary chairman of the Montreal Expos. The Expos were an expansion baseball team in the National League, and Montreal was the first city outside the United States to gain a major-league franchise. Pearson became a follower of the Expos as soon as they were established in 1969. That summer, when he travelled to Africa in the course of his work on the World Bank study, he had the scores of the Expos' games sent to him on the bottom of the World Bank telegrams he received from New York. After his appointment as honorary chairman, Pearson was an excited visitor to the Expos' 1970 spring training camp in Florida, where he delighted in having his picture taken with the players and was given a locker with his name on it.

Pearson visits the Montreal Expos at West Palm Beach, Florida, March 1970.

Pearson's various awards, already numerous before his retirement from political life, quickly increased in number. He became a Companion of the Order of Canada, received the Canadian Save the Children Fund Award and several other humanitarian awards, and increased his number of honorary degrees from universities around the world to approximately fifty. In 1971 he received a special honour when he was named by the Queen to become a member of the exclusive Order of Merit, composed of only twenty-four members. The investiture took place the following year in Buckingham Palace, where Pearson and his wife had an informal audience with the Queen. 'I expressed my sense of honour and privilege and then my wife and I just had a good chat with her,' Pearson told reporters after his thirty-minute meeting.

During these years Pearson was in great demand as a speaker. Always willing to help a cause in which he believed, he made so many speeches that he sometimes seemed to be back in public life. On the occasion of the twenty-fifth anniversary of the United Nations in 1970 he warned that the organization would diminish and ultimately disappear, 'not with a bang but on a point of order', if nations could not rise above national power, national interest, and national pride. In addition to the need to strengthen the United Nations, a frequent theme of his speeches was the necessity for wealthy countries of the world to assist the developing nations. Another, especially following publication of the Canadian government's foreign-policy review in 1970, was the warning that Canada should not yield to the temptation to withdraw into a national shell or a narrow nationalism, but should strengthen its concern for Europe, for NATO, and for the United Nations. Pearson spoke relatively rarely on purely domestic issues, but when he did he often emphasized the need for English Canadians to accept the growing aspirations of French Canada and to be receptive to proposals to promote bilingualism. By February 1970, after he had been particularly active in talking about his World Bank report, the Ottawa *Journal* observed that Pearson, 'several times a grandfather, is speaking out like a Dutch uncle. He has decided that the role of a non-talking former Prime Minister is not for him. He is becoming a forthright critic of Canadians who seem unaware of their good fortune and their responsibilities.'

In 1969 the British Broadcasting Corporation bestowed on Pearson its highest honour by asking him to give the Reith Lectures, a series of six thirty-minute radio talks. These annual addresses had been given in previous years by such renowned figures as Bertrand Russell, Arnold Toynbee, Robert Oppenheimer, and John Kenneth Galbraith. Drawing on his experience in international politics, Pearson stressed that excessive nationalism was the strongest obstacle to the building of a peaceful world community, for it made people unwilling to let 'foreigners' have any control over their own affairs. He went on to speak of the need for economic co-operation, particularly to assist the less-developed countries of the world. He proposed methods of reforming the United Nations in order to make it more effective (including a system of weighted voting that would give the larger countries a greater voice and the establishment of regional UN assemblies to deal with regional problems). The theme of his talks was the brotherhood of man and the need for international co-operation. 'We must apply the science and art of politics to the affairs of the international community with the intensity of personal involvement that we give to domesic affairs,' he said. 'We must cultivate international ideals, develop international policies, strengthen international institutions, above all the United Nations, so that peace and progress can be made secure in the family of man.'

During these years, while he delivered speeches, accepted awards, and undertook international duties, Pearson worked whenever possible on his memoirs. His goal was to tell his own story of the events with which he was associated and to present his own view of the world and its problems; he hoped to reach as wide an audience as possible, which meant that historical events would be recounted accurately but not always in exhaustive detail. With two professional historians to assist him in sorting through his innumerable files and diary notes, his task was considerably eased. But the fact that he had undertaken so many other activities meant that he was able to work on his memoirs only in his spare time. 'I have actually taken on too much,' Pearson commented in 1972. 'But when you retire, you're fair game for every good cause.'

Although the work progressed slowly, the result was worth the wait. The first volume of his memoirs, published in October 1972, rose quickly to the top of the bestseller list in Canada. The book—entitled simply *Mike*—covered the early years of Pearson's life until his entry into politics in 1948. While it did not offer much new material or many insights of interest to professional historians, it was a very human and humorous account of his life and projected his personality vividly.

Pearson was never able to devote the same time and attention to his account of the years following 1948. In 1970 he was admitted to the Ottawa General Hospital, where his right eye was removed because of a tumor. Although the exact nature of Pearson's illness was not made public, his doctors knew he had cancer. Determined to complete his memoirs, Pearson pressed on with them. By the time the first volume was published, he had done some work on the second volume (dealing with the years 1948-57), including a first chapter on his attitude towards political life, drafted sections of other chapters, and made marginal notes in research papers prepared by his historian assistants. But his strength was failing. In November the Canadian Press reported that he was suffering from 'fatigue' after a tour to promote the first volume of his memoirs and was resting at home. Knowing that he had not long to live, Pearson began work on the crucial third volume, dealing with his years in political life, since he knew that much of it could be written only by him.

In December the Pearsons flew to Florida for a holiday, but it soon became apparent that he was gravely ill. A government aircraft flew Pearson back to Ottawa just before Christmas. He was suffering from cancer of the liver and there was nothing his doctors could do. Three days later, during the evening of December 27, having lapsed into a coma, Pearson died at his Rockcliffe home.

On Saturday, December 30, four officers of the Canadian Armed Forces draped the maple-leaf flag over Pearson's coffin, which lay in the Hall of Honour of the Parliament Buildings in Ottawa. Nearby stood a wreath of poppies from the Royal Canadian Legion, which had been such a bitter opponent of the new flag in 1964. At both ends of the coffin, on small velvet cushions, rested Pearson's decorations: the Order of Merit from the Queen, the Nobel Peace Prize, the Order of Canada, and his First World War service medal. Mrs Pearson, her son and daughter, and six of her grandchildren filed by the coffin after the flag-draping ceremony, which was televised across the country. Five of the grandchildren carried

The funeral procession approaches the gravesite, December 31, 1972.

single red roses, which they laid at the centre of the flag on the red maple leaf. After the Governor General, the Prime Minister, other Cabinet ministers, and close friends had filed by, the public was allowed to pay their respects. In spite of a howling blizzard, more than 12,000 people queued outside the Parliament Buildings to wait their turn to pass by the coffin.

The funeral was held on December 31 in Christ Church Anglican Cathedral. The Prime Minister of Great Britain flew to Ottawa for the occasion: the Vice-President of the United States was also scheduled to attend but the stormy weather prevented his plane from landing. At 1 p.m. the funeral procession, led by twenty-five mounted members of the RCMP and a fifty-man escort from the Canadian Armed Forces, left the Parliament Buildings. The procession—including the Prime Minister, most of his Cabinet, and former colleagues of Mr Pearson—moved slowly westward along Wellington Street under a freezing rain to the cathedral, where an ecumenical and bilingual service was held.

Afterwards approximately thirty family members and close friends drove to the cemetery, located in the rolling Gatineau hills some twenty-five miles north of Ottawa.* Under grey and threatening skies the funeral procession crossed the Ottawa River into Québec and followed the winding highway that led through the Gatineau hills to the town of Wakefield. Then, turning onto a little-used side road, the procession passed an old stone grist mill, climbed a steep hill, and arrived at the tiny 100-year-old cemetery, surrounded by white pines and overlooking the Gatineau River. In this

---

* Almost thirty years earlier, Pearson and two External Affairs colleagues had determined that they would be buried in this peaceful little country cemetery, which they had come across during one of their hikes. Each bought a burial plot for ten dollars. In 1954 Hume Wrong was buried there, and in 1968 he was joined by Norman Robertson.

peaceful setting, in an upper corner of the cemetery beside
two of his colleagues, Lester Pearson was buried.

Following Pearson's death, newspaper editorialists and
other commentators began to assess him and his career,
particularly as Prime Minister. While some focused on his
international achievements (the Vancouver *Province* wrote:
'Mike Pearson didn't just enhance Canada's reputation as an
international diplomatic and peacekeeping force—he personally built and sustained it for many years'), most paid tribute
to his unusual human characteristics. 'There was about him
throughout his life', said the Toronto *Globe and Mail*, 'an
air of simple human decency and kindness and an unpretentious manner that made him one of the best-liked political
personalities of his time.' The Calgary *Herald* concluded that
'The most enduring of Mike Pearson's legacies may prove to
be himself, his personality, his humanity.' The Montreal *Star*
said that, while he never won complete acceptance from
Canadian voters, 'he epitomized what several generations saw
as best in our national character. The modesty, the self-
deprecating sense of humour, the intellectual stature without
intellectual pretension and the dedication to the search for
useful compromise rather than self-promotion were characteristics which many of his countrymen . . . liked to think of as
uniquely Canadian.'

Looking at his record as Prime Minister, most editorialists
considered his contribution to national unity as his greatest
achievement. The Lethbridge *Herald* said: 'Although the
Pearson years in Ottawa are remembered mainly for such
negative and unproductive things as the flag debate, there
were some substantial achievements. Probably the most
important thing undertaken was that of undergirding national
unity. Mr Pearson early perceived the need for giving the

French fact greater attention in this connection.' The Victoria *Times* commented: 'His mastery of compromise, his ability to bend with the storm, proved to be invaluable in the crucial days of French-Canadian resurgence, for stonewall tactics at that time could have been disastrous for Canada.'

For the most part, however, the record was still too recent for many definitive judgements to be reached. Historical perspective was necessary for a fair assessment of Pearson's accomplishments and failures as Prime Minister. It could be accepted at once that he had an engaging personality and had played a major part in keeping Québec within Confederation, but many questions remained unanswered. Was he a weak and vacillating Prime Minister, as the Canadian public seemed to believe during his years in power? If so, how could one explain the significant legislative record of his government? Did he really betray Cabinet colleagues such as Guy Favreau and Walter Gordon, as some memoirs and biographies suggested? Or was he not ruthless enough, as others charged, in ridding his Cabinet of ministers who had outlived their usefulness? Was his foreign policy overly subservient to that of the United States or did it maintain for Canada as much freedom as was realistic in an interdependent world?

One of the greatest Pearson paradoxes was that, while his image had been that of an indecisive, accident-prone leader, the record of his government in terms of legislation and policy was extremely impressive. The introduction of a distinctive Canadian flag and the success of Centennial Year increased Canadians' pride in their country. Canada's social-security system was significantly improved with the introduction of the Canada Pension Plan, the Canada Assistance Plan, and Medicare. The Armed Forces were unified, foreign aid was increased, and Canada's international reputation was restored.

New legislation was introduced in the field of broadcasting, labour-management relations, immigration, and transportation. Capital punishment was abolished for a five-year trial period, the penal system was modernized, and the Criminal Code was liberalized. Steps were taken to make French Canadians more at home within Confederation, including the establishment of the Royal Commission on Bilingualism and Biculturalism, the encouragement of bilingualism in the federal public service, and the acceptance of a new formula for equalization payments. Redistribution of electoral districts was undertaken, and the rules and procedures of the House of Commons were revised. Not until he had left public office did most Canadians realize the extent to which Pearson's minority government had introduced and implemented policies that were new and often imaginative.

One explanation for this contrast between Pearson's indecisive image and his impressive accomplishments is that his term in office coincided with profound changes in the social, economic, political, constitutional, and moral climate of the country. The 1960s were years of increased urbanization, a questioning of authority and traditional values, technological breakthroughs, the Quiet Revolution in Québec, the growth of nationalism in English Canada, international economic problems, and new attitudes to politics and politicians. 'Canadian politics between 1963 and 1968', wrote Peter Newman, 'was dominated by a tumble of events rather than by the personality or fate of any one man.' Pearson became Prime Minister at a time when traditional patterns of life were being challenged on all sides. It was to his credit that, handicapped as he was by serious political weaknesses, he was still able to bring about constructive changes in a time of turbulence.

This was also an era in which the Kennedy cult and the predominance of television made the personality of the party leader crucially important. Pearson was the first to admit that he was not a 'charismatic' leader. 'I could never lead a crusade, you know,' he commented on one occasion. 'I'd blush if I had to stand up and shout things like, "Follow me to the death." But I'd like to be *in* a crusade. Even in the front ranks.' Although he had been a comfortable and effective television performer in the past (notably during the tense Suez crisis of 1956), he did not possess the style or the smoothness that Canadians in the post-Kennedy years had come to expect of their politicians. He was uncomfortable with the partisan speeches he had to make, and frustrated by the fact that well-reasoned arguments often counted for little in political life. His favourite cartoon of himself was drawn by the Toronto artist Duncan Macpherson. It showed Pearson as a baseball player trying to catch a fly ball, stumbling, with his glasses and cap askew, but miraculously catching the ball, which had 'Canadian unity' written across it. He often said that he never believed in the 'no runs, no hits, no errors type of game'. Perfection is rarely attainable, either in diplomacy or in politics, and he had learned that it was wiser to compromise in order to attain part of one's goal rather than risk losing it entirely. This philosophy supported him well in political life, for it enabled him to withstand much of the day-to-day criticism he had to face.

Asked in 1966 what he believed had been his greatest accomplishment as Prime Minister, Pearson said that he had gained the deepest personal satisfaction from the adoption of the maple-leaf flag, but that his most important piece of legislation was the Canada Pension Plan, which was 'another major stage in the building of our social security structure.' Most observers, however, said that his main accomplishment was to defuse a potentially explosive situation in Québec.

Peter Newman wrote: 'No matter how history finally judges
him, there can be little doubt that Lester Pearson provided
the essential moderating influence that helped bring under at
least temporary control the centrifugal forces threatening to
split English and French Canada apart during the mid-
Sixties.' In the same vein the editor-in-chief of the Montreal
Star, George Ferguson, stated: 'It can reasonably be said
that Diefenbaker's fall and Pearson's 1963 arrival at the
summit probably saved Confederation. Pearson, his sensitive
antennae delicately tuned, knew trouble when he felt it . . . It
is no exaggeration to say that another year or two of the
Diefenbaker stand-pattism would have ended in rupture.
What Pearson gained was time, and time was all important.'

In the autumn of 1973 the second volume of Pearson's
memoirs, covering the years 1948-57, was published. Much
of it was made up of excerpts from diary notes and speeches
that Pearson had made during the major crises in which he
had been involved during these years—Palestine, Korea, and
Suez—and from interviews he had subsequently given.
Although skilfully put together by the two historians who had
worked closely with him, Volume Two clearly lacked the
personal touch that had made the first volume so delightful.
On the other hand, it contained more concrete information of
interest to historians of the period. Pearson had had little time
to work on the third volume, dealing with his years as leader of
the Liberal party, and his sudden death left the record of his
public life sadly incomplete.

In August 1973 Queen Elizabeth visited Canada on the
occasion of the Commonwealth Heads of Government meeting. While in Ottawa she officially opened the new headquarters of the Department of External Affairs, a gigantic wed-

ding-cake building stretching along the Ottawa River. Prime Minister Trudeau had announced in 1972 that the $32-million complex was to be named the Lester B. Pearson Building in recognition of his 'unique contribution to Canada's place in international affairs'. When the Queen officially opened the building on August 1, 1973, in the presence of Maryon Pearson, she noted that she had had 'the pleasure of knowing Mike Pearson for nearly a quarter of a century and greatly valued his friendship and his wisdom.' She went on to say that he had devoted his life to certain ideals and that his example had had a lasting influence on all members of Canada's foreign service. 'Naming this building after him,' the Queen said, 'will help keep that influence alive.'

This was an appropriate assessment. In spite of his contribution to the preservation of Canadian unity, Pearson's claim to a prominent place in history rests more on his record as a promoter of world order in a perilous time. He was one of the architects of the post-war system of collective security and, in a variety of capacities, the symbol of positive and constructive internationalism.

Sources and Further Reading

A major problem confronting the biographer of any contemporary public figure is the scarcity of original source material. The case of Lester Pearson is no exception. Not enough time has passed for many of the people most closely involved in various aspects of his career, particularly during his years as Prime Minister, to set down their own accounts on paper. In many cases the events are too recent and controversial and the people involved are still living, all of which has an inhibiting effect on those who were in a position to know precisely what happened. The result is that, for the time being at least, a study of Lester Pearson must rely almost exclusively on secondary sources of information—on what others have written about Pearson or the events with which he was associated. Since most do not have access to confidential material, something less than the whole story is inevitably told.

There are, however, a few original sources available, the most important of which are the two volumes of Pearson's memoirs, *Mike* (Toronto, 1972, 1973). A third edited volume is in preparation. Although incomplete, the memoirs—particularly the first volume—provide invaluable original material. Many of Pearson's most notable speeches are collected in *Words and Occasions* (Toronto, 1970), which provides a summary of his career. The most important source of information of all—Pearson's private papers—was deposited after his death in the National Archives in Ottawa. This is the information from which the record of Pearson's years as Leader of the Opposition and Prime Minister will eventually be written, but little of it is yet available to the public because of its contemporary nature. None of his private papers were used in the writing of this summary of Pearson's life.

Only a few biographical accounts have been written, none of which is very satisfactory. John Robinson Beal's *The Pearson Phenomenon* (Toronto, 1964) is the only real biography, but it ends with the year 1963. W. Burton Ayre's *Mr. Pearson and Canada's Revolution by Diplomacy* (Montreal, 1966) deals with only his first years as Prime Minister. Both books present basic factual information but are so laudatory that their objectivity is inevitably subject to question. The Liberal Federation of Canada has published a brief biographical pamphlet, *The Right Honourable Lester B. Pearson, Prime Minister of Canada* (Ottawa, 1967), which is a factual account of his life but naturally somewhat biased as well. Bruce Hutchison, in his *Mr. Prime Minister: 1867-1964* (Don Mills, 1964), has written an interesting chapter on Pearson; although primarily a character analysis, it also comments on his first year as Prime Minister.

A variety of secondary sources dealing with the period from 1919 to 1948 mention Pearson or the events with which he was associated as a diplomat. The most informative are four volumes in the *Canada in World Affairs* series: F. H. Soward *et al., The Pre-War Years* (Toronto, 1941); Robert MacGregor Dawson, *1939-41* (Toronto, 1943; C. Cecil Lingard, *1941-44* (Toronto, 1950); and Robert A. Spencer, *1946-49* (Toronto, 1959). The best accounts of the whole period between the two wars are G. P. deT. Glazebrook, *A History of Canadian External Relations, 1914-1939* (Toronto, 1942) and R. A. MacKay and E. B. Rogers, *Canada Looks Abroad* (Toronto, 1938). Another interesting account is Hugh L. Keenleyside *et al., The Growth of Canadian Policies in External Affairs* (Durham, 1960). R. Barry Farrell's *The Making of Canadian Foreign Policy* (Scarborough, 1969) contains a chapter on the growth of the Department of External Affairs, although far better on this subject is James Eayrs' *The Art of the Possible* (Toronto, 1961). J. W. Pickersgill, assisted in the later volumes by D. F. Foster, has edited four volumes of *The Mackenzie King Record,* which contain often-amusing comments by Prime Minister King about Pearson and the policies he was advocating. An account of the functions of a Canadian diplomat during these years is given by Blair Fraser in *Our Diplomats at Work* (Toronto, 1945). H. Gordon Skilling's *Canadian Representation Abroad: From Agency to Embassy* is a detailed study of the institutional development of Canadian external relations. James P. Manion's *A Canadian Errant: Twenty-Five Years in the Canadian Foreign Service* is the memoir of a former trade commissioner who occasionally mentions an anecdote concerning Lester Pearson.

Since Pearson was involved in several major international events during his years as Secretary of State for External Affairs, the sources dealing with these crises are generally detailed and of high quality. Again the *Canada in World Affairs* series provides an excellent account of the major details; by W. E. C. Harrison, *1949-50* (Toronto, 1959): B. S. Keirstead, *1951-53* (Toronto, 1956); Donald C. Masters, *1953-55* (Toronto, 1959); and James Eayrs, *1955-57* (Toronto, 1959). R. A. MacKay, in *Canadian Foreign Policy, 1945-54* (Toronto, 1971), has compiled an extensive record of the most important speeches and documents dealing with Canadian participation in many of these events. Robert W. Reford, in *Canada and Three Crises* (Toronto, 1968), discusses the 1956 Suez crisis from a Canadian perspective. The story from a wider angle is told in Mortimer Lipsky, *Quest for Peace: The Story of the Nobel Award* (South Brunswick, 1966). J. L. Granatstein (ed.), *Canadian Foreign Policy Since 1945: Middle Power or Satellite*? (Toronto, 1969), contains information on Suez as well as views on Canadian foreign policy in general in the 1950s.

The reader is also referred to three interesting memoirs written by people who were associated with various aspects of Pearson's career. The Right Honourable Vincent

Massey, in *What's Past is Prologue* (Toronto, 1963), mentions Pearson frequently in his discussion of his own years as Canadian High Commissioner in London. Arnold Heeney, the author of *The Things That Are Caesar's: Memoirs of a Canadian Public Servant* (Toronto, 1972), served under Pearson as Under-Secretary of State for External Affairs and as Ambassador to the United States. Dean Acheson's memoirs, *Present at the Creation: My Years in the State Department* (New York, 1969), occasionally mention Pearson and the disagreements the two had, particularly over Korea. In addition, the Winter 1973-4 issue of the *International Journal* of the Canadian Institute of International Affairs (subtitled *Lester Pearson's Diplomacy*) contains accounts by several Canadian, British, American, and French officials and politicians of their dealings with Pearson.

The written account of Pearson's career after he assumed the leadership of the Liberal party in 1957 is far less detailed. The events with which he was then associated are still too recent for much 'inside' information to have been revealed. One of the only accounts of this period, and by far the best source of information even if its conclusions are highly subjective, is Peter C. Newman's *Renegade in Power: The Diefenbaker Years* (Toronto, 1963). Peyton Lyon, in *Canada in World Affairs: 1961-63* (Toronto, 1968), discusses in detail the foreign-policy controversies that plagued the Diefenbaker administration and describes Pearson's attitude and approach to these issues. Patrick Nicholson's *Vision and Indecision* (Toronto, 1968) is a highly favourable account of the Diefenbaker administration. Robert Moon's *Pearson: Confrontation Years Against Diefenbaker* (Hull, 1963) is a slim volume that contributes little to the history of the period.

The major secondary source for Pearson's years as Prime Minister is Peter C. Newman's *The Distemper of Our Times: Canadian Politics in Transition, 1963-68* (Toronto, 1968). As with most contemporary histories that are based on interviews and personal impressions, not all the assessments or even all the facts can be accepted without question, but it is nevertheless the most detailed and readable account of the period available. Thomas Van Dusen's *The Chief* (Toronto, 1968) is a laudatory account of John Diefenbaker's career that also covers his years in Opposition and provides some information on the atmosphere that existed during the Pearson administration. At the time of writing only two first-hand accounts of Pearson's years in power had appeared. Judy LaMarsh, in *Memoirs of a Bird in a Gilded Cage* (Toronto, 1968), gives her impressions of the years 1963-8, during which she held two Cabinet portfolios, and arrives at critical conclusions about Pearson's leadership abilities. Denis Smith, in *Gentle Patriot: A Political Biography of Walter Gordon* (Toronto, 1973), makes use of a memoir prepared by Gordon as well as some of his personal papers to provide an account of the Pearson administration from the viewpoint of another Cabinet minister. Again some of Pearson's dealings with his Cabinet colleagues are criticized.

Because of this shortage of original material, the most important source of information for Pearson's years as Prime Minister, as well as for the last four years of his life, is newspaper accounts. While they cannot always be relied on to provide the whole story, they are the best source available at present. The Toronto *Globe and Mail*, the Toronto *Star*, the Toronto *Telegram*, the Montreal *Star*, the Montreal *Gazette*, *La Presse*, *Le Devoir*, the Ottawa *Citizen*, the Ottawa *Journal*, the Halifax Chronicle-Herald, the Winnipeg *Free Press*, the Regina *Leader-Post*, the Saskatoon *Star-Phoenix*, the Calgary *Herald*, the Edmonton *Journal*, the Vancouver *Sun*, and the Vancouver *Province* are the main Canadian daily newspapers that should be consulted for news stories and editorial comment.

A final source of information, particularly useful for ascertaining Pearson's philosophy and major concerns, is his published writing. His books dealing with international relations are *Democracy in World Politics* (Princeton, 1955); *Diplomacy in the Nuclear Age* (Toronto, 1959), which also contains his Nobel Peace Prize Lecture, 'The Four Faces of Peace'; and *Peace in the Family of Man: The Reith Lectures 1968* (Toronto, 1969). The report of the World Bank commission on international development assistance, of which Pearson was chairman, is *Partners in Development: Report of the Commission on International Development* (New York, 1969).

Index

207